MAN UP

SCOTT C. SCHULER

IT'S HARD TO RESIST A BAD BOY...EVEN MORE SO A GOOD MAN!

A POST HILL PRESS BOOK

MAN UP:
It's Hard to Resist a Bad Boy…Even More So a Good Man!
© 2017 by Scott C. Schuler
All Rights Reserved

ISBN: 978-1-68261-520-1
ISBN (eBook): 978-1-68261-521-8

Cover Design Art Direction: Justin Anderson
Interior Design and Composition by Greg Johnson/Textbook Perfect
Project Collaboration: Joanna K. Hunt

Post Hill Press
New York • Nashville
posthillpress.com

Published in the United States of America

SCOTT'S THANKS

First and foremost, thanks to my Savior for the blessings and giftings you have given to someone so unworthy. To my wife, Brenda, thank you for your never-ending patience and love as I work to be the husband you deserve. To my mom, thank you for raising me well and being a never-ending example of compassion, love, and generosity. And to the four men in my life who are the reason for this book. To my dad, thank you for being the best example I could have of what a real man is. You have modeled manly strength in love, faith, marriage, work ethic, and so much more. I am eternally grateful for your hand on my life. To my three boys, Wyatt, Garett, and Everett, my prayer is that I model the same manliness for you that my dad did for me. And finally, to two incredibly important people in my life, Randy and Robyn Murrah. Thank you for your friendship and mentorship in my life.

TABLE OF CONTENTS

Foreword by Brenda Schuler vii

Introduction xi

Chapter 1: MAN UP to Yourself 1

Chapter 2: MAN UP in the Workplace 13

Chapter 3: MAN UP in Your Health 37

Chapter 4: MAN UP as a Friend 55

Chapter 5: MAN UP in Your Marriage 75

Chapter 6: MAN UP as a Father 103

Chapter 7: MAN UP Spiritually 136

Chapter 8: MAN UP for Future Generations 155

The MAN UP Manifesto 161

FOREWORD

by Brenda Schuler

Women around the world are screaming! SCREAMING—*"Where have all the good men gone?"*

Everywhere I go, I am constantly asked about Scott, "Where did you find this guy?… Does he have a brother?"

What is it that Scott has that women are screaming for?

Scott and I have been together more than half of our lives. However, the man he is today is not the same man that I married. Don't get me wrong, I loved him then and I love him now, that part is the same. What has changed is how deep my respect for him has grown and what he overcame physically, spiritually, and emotionally to MAN UP to who he is today.

I met Scott in college. Honestly, I wasn't particularly attracted to him at first. He wasn't my type. At the time, I was casually dating and always interested in the "preppy" finance majors. Scott was, well…Scott; casual and rugged. Not terribly concerned about his appearance or what people thought of him. He sat in the back of our physiology class and slept half the time. The teacher would often give pop quizzes and Scott would wake right up, take the test, and make an A. Every. Single. Time. Of course, I was wide awake in class, studied like crazy, and still would barely make a B or C.

I was intrigued by Scott and infatuated with his brain. We had several classes together so we'd run into each other often and engage in small talk in the hall. I finally asked him to "help me study" and the rest was history. (I know—who's the smart one now?)

Scott always had such an incredible heart. He was well liked and had many friends. He was always helping people but occasionally they would take advantage of his goodness. That really bothered me because he is so loyal and protective. He was also extremely trustworthy, which was a big deal, because for me trusting wasn't always easy. I knew it was vital to any healthy relationship, yet it was so difficult to find.

Even though we were different in a lot of ways, our relationship worked because we had open and honest communication. One unique quality about Scott is his ability to get me to talk about my feelings. Yes, you read that correctly. Scott, the big, burly Renaissance man, was leading me, the outgoing, preppy, blonde girl, to talk about my feelings. You see, my dad was Norwegian and my mom was Polish. Not much "touchy feely" in my gene pool. We just didn't talk about our feelings in my house growing up. Later in life, that all changed and we became more expressive. But Scott was always great at articulating his feelings. Our fights seemed to always stem from this difference. Somehow, Scott would get me to open up because I trusted him, and I saw his character and integrity. I felt emotionally safe with him, and it created a lasting bond in our relationship.

It wasn't always "blue skies and smooth sailing" for us though. Far from it. We had lots of issues to work through as a couple. Early on, Scott had a pretty colorful temper. That manifested as severe road rage, which freaked me out every time we got in the car! This wasn't just your ordinary five-o-clock-I'm-tired road rage. This was expert level. I'm talking bumper-riding, horn-honking, California-waving and cussing out the window! He eventually overcame it, but it was a telltale sign there was a huge dissatisfaction inside of him.

Not only did he have this little anger issue, but he also had what we all now affectionately call Occupational ADD. He was a hard worker and excelled at whatever he attempted; he just didn't feel fulfilled on his career path so he would set out to find another. When we met, he was doing all his pre-reqs for vet school, then that changed to becoming a US Marshall, a program he was accepted into. Scott would have gladly laid down his life like the heroic men and women who serve every day, but that was something that I couldn't live with. He then set out to be a mechanic, then a plumber, an HVAC tech, and the list seriously goes on and on. Scott has always enjoyed learning new trades and anything that involves working with his hands. His family thought he might be more fulfilled in an office and he felt torn trying to make everyone else in his life happy. He ended up choosing chiropractic because he thought it was the best of both worlds—an office job working with his hands. And $160k later, he had his own practice.

And hated it.

He will tell more of his side of this story in this book but from my side, this wasn't a fun process. I felt the need to fill in the stability gaps in our home, which was a lot of pressure for me, and at one point, the lid blew off. We found ourselves living apart and reevaluating our relationship on every level. As difficult as this season was, it became a launching point for us in so many ways. At the end of the day, Scott needed to work on himself and rediscover what he wanted and who he wanted to be in the world; I needed to give him the space, love, and support to do so—even when I didn't want to! Scott needed to learn to stay true to himself and I needed to better voice my needs and open up about how I was feeling. And we both did. I found my voice and Scott discovered what became the basis for this book...how to MAN UP.

Today, our relationship is as strong as ever. As Scott has become more grounded in who he is as a man, our whole family has become more grounded as a whole.

There is so much more to this story that could become a book unto itself. At the end of the day, no one knows Scott better than I do. No one else has had a front row seat to watch him walk through the MAN UP process. I can tell you with 100 percent certainty, there is no one more qualified to write this book. I've watched him step up in every single area of life. He is strong and he is strong enough to admit when he is wrong. He is strong enough to do the right thing when no one is watching. He is strong enough to deal with his past. He is strong enough to put his family first. He is strong enough to stay true to his word. He is strong enough to stand up for his convictions. He is strong enough to stand up for those who cannot stand up for themselves. He is strong enough to set a goal and go after it no matter the opposition. Scott is the epitome of a real man, not because he is big and burly or hunts or rides a Harley, but because he is confident and secure in who he is. He is true to himself and he uses his inner strength in a way that benefits those around him.

As you read this book, know that you are reading words from someone who has taken the road less traveled. It is a road of humility and hard work—blood, sweat, and tears. It is a road of uncertainty and difficulty but it is also a road to an amazing destination—authenticity as a man, which is a very attractive quality!

As a wife, I am so incredibly proud of who my man is. He is an amazing provider, father, and lover. He is both the man I always dreamed of and he is the man beyond my wildest dreams. I can say wholeheartedly that you can trust his word, trust his character, and trust the journey with him to MAN UP.

To the men: I pray this book will provoke a sense of desire in you to become the best possible version of you. I want this book to give you hope that it *is* possible no matter what you have done, where you have been, or where you are now and that you are worth it. You were born for greatness! Go out and get it!

To the ladies: The revolution of strong men is coming...one is reading this book right now! Be ready to support, love, and receive him through the process. We are in this together, and we can all do this together.

God Bless,
Brenda M. Schuler

INTRODUCTION

It doesn't take long watching TV or browsing the internet before you see a man cast in the light of a bumbling idiot, controlling monster, or spineless sap. What has happened to the strong hunter-gatherer man who is not afraid to assert himself, protect what is his, open a door for someone, or stand up for others not able to stand up for themselves?

Men were different when I was a kid. I grew up on a hobby farm in the southwest corner of Minnesota in a small town of about 2,500 people called Windom. One of my grandfathers was a farmer, the other a truck driver, and my father, well he was the epitome of a man's man. If I could sum up Dad, I'd say he was a cross between Clint Eastwood and John Wayne. Dad was a businessman who trained horses after working all day. He exuded toughness. So much so, that one year he played high school football with a cast on his leg...in fact they had to replace that cast nine times. I watched him make a rank, stud horse's knees turn to rubber with a single punch when the horse went after me. I also saw him handle newborn colts, fillies, puppies, kittens, and us kids with absolute loving tenderness. I remember how he was strong in discipline yet even stronger in love when dealing with me and my sisters. He would never back down from a fight, but first and foremost, he would never start one either. Dad has and continues to love and show the deepest respect for my mom after fifty years of faithful marriage.

My life experiences influenced by strong men who molded me, combined with an entrepreneurial spirit, curious mind, and the drive to raise three boys into real men, are the catalyst for writing this book. My hope is to encourage men of all ages to take a hard look in the mirror at the type of man they are. The only way to get a clear picture of where, what, or who you want to be in the future is to get an accurate picture of where you are today. The "how to MAN UP" is different for all men, yet the struggle to do so is the same. It doesn't matter if you are single or not, or a father or not. Apply the information in this book to all of your relationships, whether it be as a husband, or to the woman you are dating, or your mother or sister, and watch them fall over in disbelief that men like you still exist!

In the chapters to follow, we'll explore the concepts of manhood as it relates to who you are as an individual, in relationships, and what it means to your future. We'll drill down specifically to see what it looks like to MAN UP in the workplace, with your health, as a friend, in marriage, and as a father. At the end of each chapter, you'll also read an interview of someone handpicked by me who I know is crushing that specific area of manhood in their life. I want you to learn their secrets of success and understand what they do on a regular basis. What are their biggest struggles? What do they do to keep on track when things get difficult? Who do they look up to as a mentor? If you are looking for a statistical book full of analytics, stop here. If you are looking for stories of success, failure, and perseverance that will help you realize that, as a man, although we are not perfect, we have a responsibility to ourselves and as fathers of men in training, to lead them along a path that gives them a chance to be the best version of men they can...I think you will find value in this book. It is time to stop apologizing for being men and trying to fit into the mold society says we should. It is time to embrace the very things that separate us from being womanlike and celebrate how men and women, wonderfully different, should complement each other, not compete with each other. I write this book, not being all knowing or having mastered the content within but as a reminder, first to myself, to always be moving forward...making imperfect progress... becoming a better man today than I was yesterday.

CHAPTER 1

MAN UP TO YOURSELF

At the end of a person's life, most often their biggest regrets are about the things they *didn't* do—the chances they didn't take, or the realization that they followed a path based on what other people thought was best instead of what they thought was best for themselves. Sometimes it's difficult to accept the fact that the life we've been living isn't our own. I had to come to this understanding myself and it took me years to do so. For a long time, I wasn't happy with my life and I just couldn't figure out why. I had some hard choices to make when I took a good look at my life and how I got to where I was. I had to MAN UP to who I was first before I could MAN UP in any other area.

What about you? How do you feel about your life today and the choices you've made? Maybe you've never, ever stopped to consider these things. If you haven't, there are some telltale signs that you aren't being true to yourself. Here are just a few of them:

You might need to MAN UP to yourself if...

- you dread going to work every day and live for the weekends.
- you are constantly short-fused and upset with those around you, particularly with the ones you love the most. (Road rage falls into this category.)
- you play more video games than a teenage boy.
- you think everything is someone else's fault. (No, it really isn't.)
- you think others owe you something.
- your first thoughts are always of yourself and what you want.
- you're constantly looking and never satisfied—if you are on the hunt for something "bigger and better." (This includes surfing the internet in "private" mode or viewing things that you need to clear out of your browser history.)

Did any of this hit home with you? Don't worry, I'm certainly not judging. I've lived a life I wasn't satisfied with either. However, we aren't meant to live in frustration, dissatisfied at every turn, and it doesn't have to be that way for the rest of your life. The good news is that once we own up and MAN UP to who and what we are, then we can start making changes.

Follow Your Own Path

Horses are my dad's passion. He has been riding and training horses since he was a kid, and for all intents and purposes he is a modern-day cowboy. When I was a young boy growing up, I went everywhere and anywhere I could with him. Even if it was a simple run to the garbage dump, I wanted to be in the passenger seat of the old Ford pickup right beside him. One of the places I remember vividly was the local tack store filled with saddles, bridles, boots, and all sorts of other gear. To this day, any time I walk into a place that sells leather goods, the aroma instantly takes me back to those times with my dad.

On one of those trips to the tack store, my dad bought me my first pair of spurs. If you are not up on your Western tack lingo, the spurs attach to your boots and are used when riding a horse to get their attention by giving them a little tickle. The rowels are little wheels on the back of the spurs that you run along the side of the horse, causing you to get said attention. The rowels are what make that sound you hear when watching an old Western movie on TV and some dust-covered, steely-eyed cowboy walks into a saloon with the telltale jingle in every step as his boots strike the floor. (If you are fancy, you have jingle-bobs on your spurs as well, which adds even more to the effect!) Back then, my first pair of spurs was a big deal for me! Misuse of spurs could mean losing control of your horse and facing serious injury. For my dad to buy me a pair meant that he trusted my judgment.

After my dad paid for my spurs and whatever else he needed that day, we hopped in the truck for the ride home. I had my new spurs in my hand and I wasn't paying attention to anything else! As I was running the rowels up and down my leg, I looked up at my dad and said, "Dad, can you imagine what I could do with these if they had a motor on them?" Looking back, Dad says it was this moment when he realized I was not going to be a horse guy like him. Clearly, I was more interested in the other kind of horsepower—machines and motorized vehicles!

I don't actually remember saying that, but one thing I do remember is that my dad never corrected me or chastised me for that statement. He didn't try to steer my natural interests. He let me forge my own path and didn't force me down his. And, unfortunately for him, he was right. I never did become a big horse guy like him. But, I always tell him I still ride horses. They just happen to be iron horses with two wheels instead of four hooves! I'm done feeding mine when I shut the key off, and I don't have to bale hay for them. It is important to follow your own path, but even more important not to force someone else down your path as well.

The Other "F" Word

People don't take chances for reasons too numerous to count. Fear is often the underlying driver—be it fear of the unknown, fear of failure, or as ridiculous as it sounds, fear of success. People wonder, "What happens if I accomplish the goal or dream? Do I want the responsibility that comes with it?" One of the jokes between me and my wife along with the rest of my family, is my struggle with OADD, which is my own acronym for what I lovingly call Occupational Attention Deficit Disorder. I have always struggled with deciding on what I wanted to be when I grew up. If I saw someone doing something that looked interesting, my thoughts were never, "I don't know how to do that." My mentality was always, "I'm going to learn and figure out how to do that!"

One evening, my wife and I sat and counted out the number of different jobs we have had since our childhood. My number came out to over thirty different jobs. Okay, let me explain. I wasn't at all a crappy employee. I have never been fired from a job or "invited" to turn in my resignation not one time in my life. However, my entire life I also never once heard my parents say, "You can't do that." I never thought twice about whether or not I could do something, I just started doing and learning it! (If you are a parent, try your hardest to never put the thought in your child's head that they can't do something.) And I am grateful for each and every crappy job I have ever had.

Trust me, every job was not because I thought it looked interesting. Many were simply because I didn't want to go hungry. Looking at the skills I use every day as an entrepreneur, there isn't one job I've had in the past that didn't prepare me in some way to do what I am doing today. Does this mean I have no fear? Not necessarily. It may just mean that I have learned to manage that fear and put it in its proper place. I don't let fear make my choices for me.

But, think about it for a minute—what is fear really? Could it be that the greatest fear is more about not having control, or losing it? I have talked about writing this book for years, yet I never did. If I am to be completely honest, it was because of fear—specifically, fear of losing control of my story. It was fear of putting myself and my deeply personal views out there for the public to weigh in on and criticize...fear of what people may think...fear of people not finding value in what I have to say. All of that is a fear based on losing control. In order to continue growing and moving forward, I needed to face those fears head-on. Without facing those fears, the chances of other fears popping up and preventing my movement grows exponentially. I love the story of Harley-Davidson and that company's rise to the top, and this quote from an old Harley ad fits well here: "When writing the story of your life, don't let anyone else hold the pen." There will always be things in life that cause us to fear, but we should never give control of our "pen" to fear or anyone else.

Move Your Assiduity

Old-time radio personality, author, and motivational speaker Earl Nightingale once said: "Most people spend more time picking out a suit of clothes than planning their careers or even their retirements." The complacency trap is real. It often looks like a comfort zone, which is merely a coffin buried six feet under the ground of the familiar. Many people who have settled on a vocation or path in life have had dreams of doing something bigger and better.

What is it that changes inside of a person and causes them to accept the status quo? I think for a lot of people it's something in that magical moment when you get home from work and simply realize how tired you are. Sometimes it's that feeling of grabbing a beer or soda and camping out on a comfortable couch in front of some sort of "frontal lobotomy machine," a.k.a. media device or television. Yes, it's easy to get comfortable in a routine and allow that temporary comfort to trump any and all of the ambition you had during the day. The discomfort you experienced during your workday, which encouraged you to dream about something bigger and better in the first place, is now numbed and forgotten and you've taken no action toward your dream. What will it take to get your assiduity moving? Assiduity is simply your determination, drive, and focus. But I think you know what other word fits here too! When all is said and done, most people take action and change for one of two reasons: if the pleasure is great enough, or if the pain is great enough. Either way, a decision will be made and change will happen. How long will it last? Change will last as long as the pleasure or pain can be remembered vividly, or until a new habit is created.

Pain can be a powerful motivator. When pain becomes a catalyst for growth, I wholeheartedly proclaim that the pain should not be forgotten! It should be highlighted and taped to the bathroom mirror, your computer monitor, *and* the steering wheel of your car. This pain is doing you a favor. Hold it closely, because it can drive you toward what you really want in life.

Pain, discomfort, and dissatisfaction in life are what drove my wife and me to sacrifice and build our business. Pain is what finally drove me to MAN UP and leave the chiropractic profession. It was painful to admit I didn't enjoy doing what I had spent years of school and $160,000 to learn. Pain was the javelin that I used for the monumental task of getting over my pride, ego, and my then false identity. Looking back, I can't imagine how crappy my life and my relationships would be now if I hadn't been able to make the leap. I was ornery and miserable, making those around me feel the same. Did I make the wrong choice when I decided to go into chiropractic? Was I doing what I truly wanted to, or was I doing it because I thought others expected it of me? I struggled with those questions for quite some time.

What I eventually figured out was that it didn't really matter. It was the past, and the decisions had already been made by me fourteen years ago. Whether I did it for the wrong reasons or simply learned I didn't like to do it anymore due to situations surrounding managed care, it didn't matter. What mattered was my decision-making process and my path moving forward.

However, please don't forget about common sense when making major decisions like this. If your job pays the mortgage and your bills, you don't march into your boss's office and quit without a strategy and financial plan in place. No amount of pain or daydreaming is worth committing financial suicide. Luckily for me, my wife had started a business from home that afforded me to make the leap. But, it also took four years of me not being happy and us working our plan to get me out of that job.

Until you are in a position to make the leap, use the pain to develop and drive your exit plan. This takes an incredible amount of a word that isn't very popular—discipline. Unfortunately, we live in a microwave society where everyone wants everything instantly yesterday. "What, you want me to be patient and wait for something?" Yes. For this, a great amount of discipline is needed, which takes focus, responsibility, and a lot of the time. Oh and by the way, it isn't much fun. I love a quote commonly attributed to Thomas Edison: "Opportunity is missed by most people, because it is dressed in overalls and looks like hard work." The truth is, being strong and disciplined in hard work takes practice. However, the more you take action on it, the easier it gets.

Remember the whole fear thing we discussed earlier? Facing our fears is one of the biggest tips on moving forward. If you do something that scares you just a little every day, do you know what will happen? Soon enough, you will find yourself doing bigger things that scare you. You will also start to notice, when things come at you out of the blue that would have normally scared the crap out of you, facing them head-on doesn't seem so challenging anymore.

If you have been paying attention so far, you may be thinking, "Ha, I got him! Aren't I supposed to be putting my family's needs before my own?" Of course, a big part of manning up is the understanding that our actions affect more than just us. This is where the discipline piece really kicks in. If you are unhappy because you never did follow your dreams, it doesn't give you permission to go on a sixty-day journey to the Himalayas to find yourself—unless of course, your wife is a saint. Manning up means going after what you want on your *own* time, not your kids' time, and not your wife's time. Is it tough? Of course it is, but *your* choices in life have led you to where you are, and *your* choices and actions are what can get *you* to where *you* want to be.

Embrace the Suck

My trainer has a phrase that he uses while kicking my butt at the gym. He says, "Embrace the suck, Scotty. It's the only way you will ever reach your goals!" It's specifically for those times when I am used up, spent up, out of breath, and wondering if the torture is really worth it. This is definitely one of those instances when you must learn to embrace the suck! In fact, one of the ways you know you are on the right path to your purpose is when embracing the suck doesn't seem so bad anymore. When you've reached the point where you can enjoy the blood, sweat, and tears portion of this process, you know you are on the right path. The blood, sweat, and tears are the late nights and early mornings, when everyone else is sleeping, but you are up embracing the suck and going after your dreams. You understand, that you must temporarily set aside some of the fun things, or playtime, in order to go after what's bigger and better.

This is an important piece, especially if you have kids. Our kids deserve to see us going after what we want, facing our fears and working hard to make things happen. If all they see is a depressed lump that sits on the couch, pissed off, because of the choices they have made in life, what kind of message do you think it sends to them? What kind of expectations do you think they are going to grow up with? It is our job to be the rock for them. They need to see us leading the way, taking control of life, and embracing the suck if and when necessary. They should be able to clearly see that we are the only one holding the pen while writing our book.

And speaking of writing a book, this book wouldn't have been possible if it hadn't been for inspirational "guru" Gary Coxe who challenged me to "embrace the suck" and actually write this book! He is appropriately the first interview.

MAN UP to Yourself: Interview with Gary Coxe

Scott: When I say "man up in life," what does that bring to the forefront of your mind?

Gary: Don't let little or big things knock you down. When you do get knocked down, quickly get right back up!

Scott: How many years have you been an entrepreneur?

Gary: I started when I was eleven. About forty years.

Scott: What's been your favorite experience as an entrepreneur?

Gary: I'm obsessed with the challenges! I like to have an idea and then work hard and watch it come to light.

Scott: What's been the biggest struggle for you as an entrepreneur?

Gary: The emotional roller coaster. I risk, I push, I work so hard. You have to manage the emotional ups and downs, which can be a challenge when you are aware of the fact that not everything is going to work out the way you hoped all the time. But payoff always comes.

Scott: So would you say that being an entrepreneur isn't all roses, and just like any other relationship, or area of life, those emotions have the potential to derail you?

Gary: No question about it! There's nothing more challenging and nothing that will stretch you and make you a better human than being an entrepreneur. Or being a successful entrepreneur, let's put it that way.

Scott: What has been your main motivation to succeed or achieve excellence?

Gary: I'm just obsessed with trying to do things better. I'm obsessed with mastering my mind because if you master your mind, you master everything. You master motivation, you master drive, you master kindness, you master charity, you master you. I think self-mastery has been a huge motivation for me. If I have a thought that makes me lazy or demotivated, I haven't mastered my mind, especially if I reward that thought with action. I also believe I'm on this planet to help remove pain from people. That's a huge motivation for me.

Scott: We have talked in the past about the importance of action as an entrepreneur, as a person in business, as a man who is gonna say, "Alright, I'm takin' this to the next level." What are your thoughts when you hear the word "action"?

Gary: My thought is that action equals results. You want more results or want them more quickly, then you have to take more action. I am obsessed with execution, which means I can get an idea and I do something with it immediately, even if it's just to write it down so I don't forget it. So when you have an idea, it may be for next year but you have to start doing something about it now. Execution is huge. I think many people don't really get what execution means. They don't see the sense of urgency so if people say they want more results in any area, then it's all about execution and how fast execution becomes a process of our mind. How fast can we get to the point where we're always executing when we're on?

Scott: Do you think people tend to have misconceptions on what execution or taking action actually entails? Do you think it needs to be a huge, detailed plan, or can it just be something really simple to start the process moving forward?

Gary: Absolutely, because execution to me might be just putting seven things down on a to-do list. I've very action-oriented. When people hang around me, they know exactly what that means to me. It's move, get things done, next, next, next, next, next. I think people become insular. They get so stuck in their own little world and their own thoughts that when they see a higher standard of excellence or a higher standard of execution, then it's kind of like watching the Road Runner lap Wile E. Coyote. You don't realize how slow you're going until that guy just passes you! It's important to find people who are moving faster than you and have higher standards and accomplish more than you do. That helps sharpen your focus so you can understand what movement and execution are needed to get results.

Scott: On that note, I've heard the phrase, "Are you playing big?" I get that phrase, but the way I look at it is that in order to play big, first you have to think big. How important is thinking big, and what do you think stops people from thinking bigger?

Gary: Good question. A lot of times people try to "go big" but they don't have the belief system in place to support the concept. They think it's about something huge—and it could be—but they're not doing little things right now to get to the big things. They don't have the daily goals to little tiny day-by-day, chip, chip, chip, chip, chip away with that big thing in mind. So what happens is we're in one place and have a goal in another place. Many times there is a gap between the two places. In that gap there is a lot of discouragement, struggles, challenges, and obstacles along the way. So instead of taking little things toward that goal, they try to make a big leap and the discouragement in the gap is too high so they just cave in and don't worry about it anymore. Then they just get stuck in their little own world.

Scott: Here's a phrase I just love: "Nice guys finish last." Do you think there's any truth to that in business, or do you think that you can still be a nice guy and crush it in business?

Gary: No question, but this is where I think a lot of people don't do well in business, because they don't have a balanced viewpoint of nice. Sometimes people go overboard when they have to say something to somebody and they think that person may perceive them as not being nice, but as long as you know in your right mind that you're firm yet kind, that's where the difference is. There may be a situation you have in your company. I had a situation with an assistant I had for seven years. I hated to let her go, but I told her, "As the company grows, the company is going to run over you unless you change your thought process and your beliefs and move ahead." When I let her go, there was no need to let her lose her dignity or anything. I just said, "I think we're at the point where we've come to our ends together."

What happens often in business is that a guy's ego will get in the way. Somebody will piss a guy off from a man's standpoint, and instead of handling the situation with kindness, they'll chew 'em out or yell at 'em or whatever, instead of being firm but kindly. I believe in praising in public and counseling in private so it's rare that I will counsel or correct in front of other people.

Scott: What do you think stops most men from trying to move forward in their careers?

Gary: Well, ultimately, it's their thinking—but it's fueled by the story they tell themselves. They've got a reason they're telling themselves why they can't or they shouldn't do it. People either justify, shift the blame, or minimize it. One of those three things is going on in our head that keeps us, I think, from manning up. We're shifting the blame, we're blaming it on our past, something happened to us. We're minimizing it, "Oh, there's no need for me to do that," or we're justifying why we can't do it.

Scott: So in essence, what you're saying is that in order to man up, we really need to be honest and put some critical thought into our lives and where we're at and why we're doin' what we're doin'?

Gary: Yeah, and look for those three things that you're buying into that are keeping you from doing what you should be doing or would like to be doing more of.

CHAPTER 2

MAN UP IN THE WORKPLACE

As I write this, my dad is approaching his seventy-first birthday and he still has more stamina than most men half his age. He is a cancer survivor, broken too many bones to count while training horses, his knees are shot, he's had two back surgeries and another on the way, not to mention he has virtually no feeling in his hands and feet. Yet, I would put him up against almost any other younger man out there and he would work them into the dirt! His work ethic is one I have yet to see matched anywhere. As I thought about what it means to MAN UP in the workplace or in business, I thought of him and this is what came to me: How badly do you want it? How badly do you want the promotion, success, money, security, or whatever it is you are dreaming about? How much effort are you willing to put in to get it?

As part of our business, my wife and I coach individuals and entrepreneurs who want to make it to the top. The phrases "I'm trying" or "I'm doing my best" are like fingernails on a chalkboard to me. Plain and simple, these are excuses to avoid explaining why someone has fallen or is falling short of their goals. Either you do or you don't; there is no in between. (Yoda said it best: "Do or do not. There is no try.") If you aren't advancing forward, or at the very least making imperfect progress, you are sliding backwards. Examples of this principle are all around us. Trees, flowers, even we as human are either growing or dying, it's never just trying or existing.

I hear all the time, "I'm doing my best." What does that even mean? I have been able to achieve great success in life. I don't say this to brag, but to make a point. I don't know if I have honestly ever given my absolute 100 percent best. You know, completely gassed, left everything in the ring, tank is empty, I've got nothing left to give type of best. This notion hit me one day when I sent a text message to a friend of mine who was a former member of an elite military group. After four or five days, I finally heard back. But this message was certainly not like anything I had ever received before and most likely never will again. It simply said, "Scott I'm at survival school for another week. I was just in a cell the size of a school locker for the past five days. When I get back, I'll hit you up."

You know those Jet.com commercials where the top of the shopper's heads blow off in spectacular color? That's how I felt when I read his message. There are people who have given their ultimate best, and if that's you, feel free to proceed to the next chapter. The rest of us have some more work to do. My point is, most of us have never tapped into what we are truly capable of. Why is that? Why do we settle for less? What is it that drives us to do what we do? Are you blissfully happy where you are now in your career? If yes, and you've reached the pinnacle of success and crushed your goals, thank you for reading my book this far, and by the way, can we talk later? I am elated for you, and you may proceed to the next chapter. But if you are like the other 99 percent of the population, what is stopping you from achieving your goals?

Does any of the following sound familiar: "You don't understand, I have kids...I don't have a high enough education level...I don't have enough money...I have too much debt...I have a disability...I have nothing but bad luck...My boss has it out for me...I'm waiting for the right opportunity...." Have you ever used one of these phrases? You do realize these are nothing but excuses for failure or excuses for not trying, right?

I have heard all of these multiple times, and even said some myself. I probably should have disclosed this at the beginning of the book, but I did not write this book to blow smoke up anyone's backside. I'll say it again: each and every one of those answers is simply an excuse. Until you are able to admit you're making excuses, you will never realize your full potential and be able to actually "give your best." Guess what? Giving your best is actually pretty easy when you think about it. Your best may not be that much now but each time you give your best, your best gets a little bit more. Hmmm...sounds a lot like imperfect progress.

Find the Value of Why

Your reason for wanting something or giving your best is called your "why." Simon Sinek wrote a great book, *Start with Why: How Great Leaders Inspire Everyone to Take Action*. If you are struggling with excuses, MAN UP, get the book, read it, and apply it. The reason you must start here is simple. Your current "why" is not strong enough for you to take consistent action to go after what you want. Until your "why" is one that you place enough value on, you'll never get what you want.

Let's go through a little visual exercise I use with the people. If I put a ten-foot-long two-by-four board on the ground and tell you I will give you $1,000 to walk across that board without falling off, would you do it? Of course you will "try" it for a thousand dollars! Next, I add some stipulations. A fall equals a fail, and if you fall, you owe me twenty dollars. Would you still do it? Hmmmm, lose twenty bucks or gain a thousand, most likely you still would give it a try.

Now, let's ramp up the stakes a little. We place the same two-by-four between two buildings, sixty feet in the air. Would you still cross for a thousand dollars? A few adventurous or desperate souls may try, but the number of takers will drop dramatically.

This time, however, imagine yourself on the roof of one building and as you look across to the other building you see that it's on fire. Not only is it on fire, but there on the roof is your child. With the flames advancing toward your child, do you cross between the two buildings to save them?

Of course you are crossing! There would be no watching. You are either going to succeed or fail, and your child's life hangs in the balance. That is the definition of something having enough value to take a risk. *The degree of value determines the level of risk you are willing to take.*

Think for a bit on this next sentence: our thoughts dictate our emotions, our emotions control our actions, and those actions determine the results. Your thoughts and emotions place a value on your possible actions, which ultimately determines the action you are willing to take or ignore, and give you the results, good or bad. Most of our battles are won or lost between the ears. You are the only one who has the ultimate control over where it all starts—your thoughts. You must be diligent and aware of your thoughts at all times.

Guard Your Inner Circle

Your inner circle is the group of people in your day-to-day life who are closest to you and influence you the most with their words and actions. Depending on who is allowed in your inner circle, there is potential for great or catastrophic influence. These inner circles should not have a door like most shopping centers that opens automatically when someone gets close enough throwing their weight around. The door should be manned (see what I did there?) like an expensive hotel, with a doorman posted. Just because someone wants in doesn't guarantee they are getting in, and just because someone wants your headspace doesn't mean they are going to get it!

In your business circle, you should surround yourself with people who are smarter than you. They should be people who are going to challenge you to be better, hold you to your word, and care enough to call you on the carpet when you need it. Can it be painful? It can and it will be at times, but these pains are integral to growth. (Remember...embrace the suck!) There's an old saying that applies to business as much as it does to your personal life—"You are the average of the five people you hang around the most." Who are you hanging around the most while at work? What do the conversations usually sound like? In my case, if the conversations are more about discussing ideas than discussing people (gossip), the "doorman" lets them into one of my inner circles. You must be vigilant—no one else is going to guard the doors to your inner circles. I can't stress enough how important this is!

Properly Promise and Over-Deliver

I've heard and used this phrase many times in the past—under-promise and over-deliver. However, as I began to think more about the words I was using, the whole conscious language piece, I had a change of heart toward this phrase. I no longer use it, and it actually irritates me. Think about it—the phrase actually encourages deception and doing just enough to get by. To under-promise and over-deliver means you must first go to the effort of figuring out what you think is actually possible. Then, commit to a level below your capability and exceed that just enough to make yourself look good. The MAN UP mentality is to first figure out what level you think is possible with maximum commitment, commit to it, then blow it out of the water.

Own It Like a Boss

Mirror, mirror on the wall, if you're not a vampire there's always a reflection. However, these days people don't want to see it and they don't want to own it. There is a serious lack of ownership everywhere these days. Whether it is in politics, business, relationships, or life in general, it seems no one is to blame for anything! It's the "not my fault" era. Everyone knows someone else somewhere else is to blame for everything that happens. We don't live in some magical dimension where sorcerers wave magic wands and things fall naturally into place. No matter what you think of yourself, when you look in a mirror it doesn't lie. The mirror only reflects what is there.

You might remember a *Saturday Night Live* skit with the character Stuart Smalley. In the skit he sits in front of a mirror and recites the affirmation, "I'm good enough, I'm smart enough, and doggone it, people like me." Great for Saturday night comedy, not so good for personal development advice. When you think about it, the whole concept of this technique is flawed, unless you are already a sociopath. The problem? It's basically saying to lie to yourself until you believe it. But, what if you are the only one who believes people really like you? What if you really aren't good enough? What if you really aren't smart enough? Life is not fair, and not all of us are going to be the good-looking one, smart one, or good enough all the time. It's time people start taking ownership of who and where we really are in life.

Can those things be changed? With consistent action they can, but not by sitting in front of a mirror lying to ourselves. We as men need to be honest about what is reflecting back at us in the mirror, and own our missteps or failures. This is key in business, but it applies to every other part of our lives as well. By taking ownership of where we fall short and our responsibilities, it allows us the chance to grow respect for ourselves. Whether we admit it or not, falling short slowly eats away at our soul. Although taking ownership can be painful, it also comes with a smidge of self-satisfaction for doing the right thing. Not only that, it gets easier the more you do it.

People notice rare and shiny gems. Much like these gems, those who take ownership are rare and tend to get noticed and become more respected. Lastly, taking ownership gives you potential to change. Remember, each time you do, it gets easier. Bad decisions attract bad things into our lives and good decisions result in good outcomes. Ultimately, choices and change are only up to you, no one else. What do you want your reflection to look like?

Be Grateful and Humble

Former legendary basketball coach John Wooden was respected for his insight into life. Here is one of his great quotes: "Talent is God-given; be humble. Fame is man-given; be grateful. Conceit is self-given, be careful." Much like taking ownership, gratefulness and humility are rare and get noticed. Take a moment right now and think of people you know who have shown gratefulness for your help or input. Now, think of someone you went out of your way for who never expressed any form of gratitude. If both of those people asked for help again, I'm guessing one would get a yes and the other an excuse for why you were busy.

In business, the ability to call on people who are willing to lend a hand or advise you has the potential to make or break you. The more you show gratitude and humility, the greater the pool of people you have to choose from when you need help. The best way to gauge your gratefulness and humility is to look at people's response when you ask for help. Are they saying yes, or are you amazed at how busy people are when you ask for help? If people always have an excuse or are busy, it's time to take a long, hard look at this area of your life.

Keep Your Eye on Your Bobber

About a year ago my oldest son (the very one who took a crap in the yard one time...he's come a long way) said something profound when we were fishing on vacation. I was explaining to him why he should not tattle on his brothers and to worry about his own stuff that needed tending to. I asked him if he understood what I meant, and his reply stunned me. This was the response of a ten-year-old: "I think I get it, Dad. It's kinda like fishing: *you have to keep your eye on your own bobber.*" I asked what that meant to him. He replied, "Well, if you're always looking at other people's bobber, you'll miss when yours goes down, and someone else may catch your fish."

And there you have it. (Maybe he should have written this book!) Part of manning up means that your only competition should be with who you were yesterday...or in the wisdom of a ten-year-old, keep your eye on your own bobber. Your competition is not Bob, Jim, Sam, Joe, Andy, or any other person you can think of. Comparison breeds contempt, jealousy, and bitterness. It slows you down and prevents personal growth. In our business, there is a phrase we use often: "Your business will only grow as fast as you do."

In this age of the internet, opportunities to learn for free are endless. Most of us have financial budgets for different areas of our lives. There are personal budgets for food, entertainment, vehicles, and vacations. For a business, the budget may include marketing, research and development, and payroll to name a few. When it comes to budgets, part of your planning should include a personal growth budget. Your family budget or business budget should grow as your income or business grows, and so should your personal development budget.

Before we go any further, let me make explain something. Not so long ago, my philosophy of personal growth/improvement was vastly different than it is now. I was the guy who thought the people doing this were weak and needed a freaking cheerleader. I saw and continue to see so many people who have bookshelves full of this stuff. The problem is the lack of action and implementation on what they have read.

When I first started working on my personal growth, the free stuff was my best option. As the business grew, we could afford the opportunity to hire coaches and mentors as well. I've been lucky enough to spend time having a meal with, picking the brains of, and being coached by renowned motivational leaders such as John Maxwell, Andy Andrews, and Bob Proctor. That didn't happen in the beginning; the budget had to grow for that to happen. To be honest, I wasn't ready for the likes of them early on either. Each time I got a new coach or a new book, I learned something I didn't know before, or at the very least, something was reinforced that I had forgotten. All of my mentors have taught me something that I was able to implement that moved me forward in business or life.

In our business, my wife and I endeavor to teach those we are mentoring everything we know. When you are teaching someone, if you combine your knowledge with everything they know, you have someone who is effectively smarter than you. In the network marketing business, this is the leverage we strive for. Your goal with your coach, mentor, or books you are reading is to get all the information you can so you can get to the place you want to be. When you feel you have gotten everything you can from them, it is time to up your game and look for a new coach, mentor, or book. The feeling of "I've arrived, I've got this" is like cancer to your business or career. If you are willing to observe and listen carefully, everyone you meet has the potential to teach you something.

Notice I said *potential* to teach you something. You won't always learn something from everyone you meet, and it may not be as much of a lesson about what you should do but a lesson on what you shouldn't do. How many times have you, as a customer, had a bad experience with someone else's business? The lesson there is how *not* to treat your customers, or other people in general. Lessons are all around us; it's up to us to be aware when the opportunity arises, learn from it, and most importantly to take action on it.

Do You Love What You Do or Just Do What You Do?

Ambition is the strong desire to do or achieve something with determination to be successful. So, what is it that you want? I mean, what is it you really, truly desire? This is a topic where you need to be completely honest with yourself. Without total honesty, you will end up existing, not living.

John Maxwell has a great discussion on the three Rs of figuring out the difference between a job, what you do well, and your passion. R number one is *Required*. This is the job you do that pays the bills. You may not like it, but if it allows for you to be financially stable, you do it anyway. R number two is *Return*. Some activities you may find give you a greater return on your investment that others. This refers to something you can do that yields a higher income than just what is required. You're good at it, you get paid well for it, but you may not necessarily enjoy it. The third R is *Reward* It's your passion, what you love to do, and it fills you up every time you do it. There intangible benefits to this work beyond just getting a paycheck. However, unless you are independently wealthy or have a great trust fund, you can't live off of the intangible reward. If you are following your passion and it doesn't pay the bills, keep your day job. Do what's required always.

If you are stuck in the *Required* zone and you don't like it, do not jump ship without a plan in place to make the transition to the *Return*

21

zone where you start increasing your value in the workplace. The *Required* piece that pays the bills should be in place until the *Return* piece is well established.. *Reward* may simply be a hobby that the *Return* either funds, or allows you freedom of time to pursue. Now, here's the giant unicorn: When the *Return* and *Reward* are one in the same. This is where you're being paid well to pursue your passion.

Be careful what you wish for though. I know many guys whose passion was fishing (*Reward*), and they tried to make it their *Return/Required* by venturing into the guiding business. I asked one friend, "So how do you like guiding? You must love it since you get to go fishing every day." His response kind of took me by surprise. He said, "It's okay, but the only problem is, I fish less now than I did before. I spend the day helping other people catch fish, and the fun is gone." For many who attempt this, their *Reward* becomes nothing but the *Required*.

The Difference Between Excellence and Failure Is One Small Moment

There is a stark difference between excellence and success. Success is achievement based on comparing your outcomes to others or other's expectations. Excellence is achievement based on comparison of your current self to your former self. Darren Hardy, in his book *The Compound Effect*, talks about *small, seemingly insignificant choices*. Over time, these small, insignificant choices add up to big results, either good or bad. A compounding effect could be simply choosing to spend twenty minutes in self-development time versus twenty minutes watching TV. Over time, the choice of TV or self-development will shape your thinking and mold your outlook on yourself and in business. No dramatic fireworks, no bells and whistles, just consistent change.

When I was still in chiropractic practice I often heard a comment similar to this: "I don't know how this happened, I used to be thin and all of a sudden, I hit my thirties and I'm overweight." The problem was, it wasn't "all of a sudden." It was the compound effect of each small, seemingly insignificant choice they made. Things like, "I'm going to skip my workout today; I've got way too much to do," or, "It's been a long day and I don't feel like cooking, I'll just pop a pizza in." Over time these bad choices get easier and easier to make, and the results of these decisions add up. It doesn't matter what area of life we are talking about either. This applies as much to business/personal growth as it does to being a husband, father, or person of faith.

Persist Against All Odds

Pioneering self-help author Napoleon Hill said, "The majority of men meet with failure because of their lack of persistence in creating new plans to take the place of those which fail." This is the "How badly do you want it?" piece. Do you truly want to achieve excellence, or do you just like the sound of it as it crosses your lips? A phrase I hear often is, "Plan your work and work your plan." This is great, as long as your plan is the correct one.

The following process has served me, and others, well: plan, do, review, revise. Let's break that down…

- **Plan:** Take time to think through and make your plan. You wouldn't take a road trip or vacation without making some sort of plan. Why would you put more effort into a vacation than your profession? This means setting aside dedicated time for working *on* your business, not *in* your business. It's the act of giving yourself permission to take time in strategic thinking about actions that will move you toward a goal.

- **Do:** Achieving anything takes action. If you want to eat, you need to go to the grocery store, get to the refrigerator, or spend time preparing a meal. Going hungry would be the result of non-action, which could also be the result of nonaction in business.

- **Review:** Is your plan working? Do you even have metrics in place allowing you to measure progress? Without a review process, you have no way of seeing if you are even making progress, much less if the progress is in the right direction and at the correct speed to meet your goals.

- **Revise:** This step is paramount for achieving the time line of your goals, eliminating parts of the plan that are not working and adjusting the plan to meet your goals in a timely manner. In the beginning this will be a foreign concept and most likely take some time. However, with practice this becomes easier and eventually, you will find yourself naturally assessing your progress and actions throughout your day versus once a week, month, quarter, or year.

This correlates highly to your level of discipline. If you struggle with discipline you will struggle with the process of plan, do, review, revise. If you are truly struggling in this area, you do not place a high enough value on yourself and/or your goals and you need someone to help you through that process and hold you accountable. Look for someone who is doing well in business or their career and ask them to hold you accountable. You'd be surprised how many people would be honored to know that's how you view them. Sometimes you need to start small and give yourself a win. Start out with a simple plan, maybe only one action item. Do it, then review it and revise if necessary. Once you are able to master one thing, add in another. This will give you confidence and be less overwhelming than facing fifteen pages of action items and spreadsheets. If your results are not the ones you want, exactly like the plan, do, review, revise process above, you must go back to the planning phase, or in this case your thoughts.

Never Get So Busy Making a Living You Forget to Make a Life

Ambition and forward thinking are great and necessary things to advance your business or career. However, as men we must be careful we are not only looking to the future, but also enjoying the present. It is a balancing act, and we must be okay with having accountability from someone we trust in this area. Someone who will not tell you what they think you want to hear, but what you need to hear, can be instrumental in keeping us grounded. Without this piece, it is extremely easy to get hung up on continually reaching for the proverbial pie in the sky or chasing the dangling carrot. This results in often missing out on some of the most important things in life. If we go through life looking through binoculars at what's way out in front of us, we don't see the needs of our spouse and family at our feet.

People often forget, money can add headaches just as easily as it can comfort. If you are doing what is needed to provide for and/or contribute to the comfort of your family, and everyone is healthy, happy, and enjoying life, you have reached a good place. There is no amount of money that will make it any better than it is. Will more money allow you to do a few more things or fulfill some wants? Sure it will, and there is nothing wrong with that. But, if your relationships with your wife and kids are already a hot mess, more money often only equals, more problems.

MAN UP in the Workplace: Interview with D. Gary Young

Scott: Gary, give just a little background for the readers on where you started and where Young Living is now.

Gary: Well, Scott, in some ways, when I think back, it's almost like it's a dream. I don't spend much time looking back, and I don't spend much time thinking back, but when I do because somebody asked me a question, or we reminisce like we always do a little bit, it's like it's a dream.

It was a tough start, you know. Number one, nobody had ever marketed essential oils in the world before outside of the perfume, fragrance, and flavoring industry. It had never been marketed, and when I talked to people about it, they just laughed at me, said, "You're crazy. You can't market something like that." So there was no real support. Even the person I was married to at that time thought absolutely just no, this is crazy.

Of course, building a business nowadays is not like it used to be in the old days. You know, in the old days, all it took was tenacity and grit and you could build a business, but now all the rules and regulations and compliance stuff that you've gotta go through, it's a lot of money, and I didn't have the money. It was just work, and I was a one-man band for two years. Take the phone call, package the order, ship it out, mop the bathroom, fill the peanut bin after filling all six orders for the day. Then get on a plane Friday afternoon and fly out to Dallas or Kansas or wherever and do meetings for the distributors, you know, all twenty of 'em. I would get out where I could do a meeting on Friday evening, and then I'd take a flight or a lot of times I would drive. Sometimes, Nancy and Eldon would meet me, and then they would drive me to the next town so we could do a meeting Saturday morning and then the next town to do a different meeting or a meeting in a different town Saturday evening, and then another one Sunday morning and then get on a plane and fly back home to take orders Monday morning. It was a challenge, and while I was doing this, I was also trying to build St. Maries at the same time [the Idaho location of the company's first farm and distiller], and there was no support from anybody around me.

I eventually grew to where I had two employees after the second year, and they also would just look at me and say, "You're crazy. This is not gonna happen." I think there's a lot of that sort of thing that goes on in everybody's life, and I really believe that's why a lot of people will have an idea and mature it to a point of starting and then quitting. Because they get the outside feedback—"You can't do it...it won't work...this is stupid...you're better to be working a 9-to-5 job"—and they give you all this justification. Because we're human, we like other people's approval so our way of getting that approval is by listening to what they say, and that was where it was different for me. I didn't really care what their opinion was, because they weren't doing it for the reason that I was. It wasn't their project, and they didn't know what I was doing anyway so why listen to somebody tell me I can't do it? So I just turned a deaf ear to it and just kept working, and yeah, it was harder. It was a lot of sleepless nights.

Scott: So you started off, and I know some of the history of the company because I'm part of the company, and it started out on a quarter-acre plot in Spokane. Where is Young Living now?

Gary: Well, we have fifteen farms around the world now. Scott, I've lost track of how many acres we're actually farming, but I know it's well over 20,000 with wildcrafting and over 100,000 with trees and botanicals in Croatia and Ecuador. It's huge, and monetary wise, it went from a little company in Spokane, Washington, where our biggest month in Spokane before I moved was $80,000, now our biggest month, $120,000,000.

Scott: That's an incredible, mind-boggling number. You had mentioned you had twenty distributors. How many distributors do we have now in Young Living?

Gary: Two million worldwide.

Scott: So now I think people are getting an idea of why I've chosen you for this chapter of the book, to know what it looks like to man up in business. You and I have had a little bit of talk over the years about the state of men today, what we are becoming and have become. When I say "man up in business," what does that bring to the forefront of your mind?

Gary: Well, number one, to man up is to know who you are. Every one of us has our own individuality and personality, our own ideals, dreams, visions, whatever. But the man up part is having the guts to stand up against all opposition and persevere when you're being told you're crazy.

Scott: So, it doesn't really necessarily mean that I've gotta be ruthless in business. There's that saying out there, "Nice guys finish last." What does that mean to you in business? Because, quite honestly, I've been around you, and you're kind of a nice guy.

Gary: Well, thank you.

Scott: Obviously, you haven't finished last.

Gary: Yeah.

Scott: What do you think of when somebody says, "Well, nice guys just finish last"?

Gary: Well, I think the person who made that comment was jealous of a nice guy, but it's not, in my opinion, a true statement. You know, nice guys finish wherever their passion's at, and if it's last, it's because their passion was lacking, but a man that lives his life based on honesty and integrity, he can choose where he wants to finish. He can choose what he wants to accomplish and at what speed he wants to accomplish it. It's not about finishing last or, "Because I'm a nice guy I'm timid or a slacker…I sit back and I let people walk on me." That's not what it is at all. The best businessman in the world can still be a good man, and unfortunately, in our business world you don't see a lot of that.

Scott: You're saying a nice guy can still be strong in his convictions, strong in who he is, in his morals and his beliefs, and still be a fierce competitor?

Gary: Yeah.

Scott: Let's talk about motivation. I mean, to get where you've gone obviously takes some sort of motivation and takes some kind of action. What has motivated you and spurred you into action to get to where you are today? I think that part of manning up is understanding that piece.

Gary: Yes, it is. Scott, a lot of it for me is intuition. I think that in order for any man to step up to the plate and go against the odds, so to speak, or do what other people look at as the impossible, it's all about them and what their dream is and do they believe in themselves. I have a couple of motivational factors, and one was that I didn't want to ever live the way I was raised. I didn't want my kids to live the way I was raised. I didn't want them to experience life the way I did. I felt there was more to life. I had a different philosophy, perhaps, a different belief. I don't believe, as a lot of Christian people do, that God sent me here to be punished. I believe that He sent me here to achieve my full potential, but it was up to me to walk that out. He didn't say it was gonna be easy, but He said it would be worth it. And so there were a lot of factors involved.

What made the difference for me is that I would look at something. Like the essential oils, when I first discovered them in 1985, the real oils, not the perfume stuff that I got introduced to in 1978, but the real oils in Geneva at the university. When I experienced that for the first time, I just felt that it was a gold mine. It was something that God had given us, and why it had never been mined, I don't know, but that's why I said the intuitive part was my motivation. I just felt intuitive. I didn't know enough to really make an intelligent decision. I just felt in my gut, in my heart, this was the right direction to go. The opposition was horrible, it was horrible, but once I made up my mind that this was the right direction for me, to heck with everybody else!

Then I started studying it. I wanted to learn and know everything there was to know about essential oils. That's why I traveled to Turkey and studied GCMS (Gas-chromatography and mass spectromity), and I volunteered for years in the fields in France and in Egypt learning to plant, cultivate, grow, harvest, and learning distillation. I did not feel that I could make a good decision unless I knew everything that I could learn. So part of it was to learn, to research, to study.

Scott, if you were going to go buy a new chiropractic practice, let's say. You wouldn't just walk in and write the guy a check. You would want to look at his books, you'd want to look at his client flow, you'd want to look at the fallout, you'd want to look at the retention rate. You'd go through every aspect before you decided whether or not you are going to buy that practice. There was nothing for me to look at so I had to go find it one piece at a time. But the blessing of that is that it was part of my education. Every time I would go and work in the distillery in France or Egypt, the two main places, I would get more passionate about it because the intuitive feeling just got more intense. Then when I would go and study the GCMS aspect and analyze the chemistry part of it, I would get more excited again. So when you're on the right track and you start studying and researching, that will convince you that you're on the right track and your passion will grow equivalent, so it's study, research, learn all there is about it, and then start putting together a plan.

This is where I see people lose it. They'll get excited, they'll study it a little bit. They'll say, "Ah, maybe I'll try it." Then they delve into it for a little bit and think, "Oh, this is quite a bit of work, you know, maybe it's not quite what I thought it was going to be." Then they start doubting themselves and questioning everything, and they quit. When you have a dream and you have a passion and you have an idea that has value; for me, it also has to have value for the people in the world. I couldn't get passionate about something just for myself, but when I could see the value it had for the world, it drove the passion. People would say, "Well, Gary, did you get excited?" and I said, "Yeah, I got excited," but there is a difference between excitement and passion. Excitement is like the igniter on a propane stove. You hold the button down, you strike the match, and the little pilot light comes on. That's excitement. But as soon as you take your thumb off it, the pilot light goes out, but if you hold your thumb on it long enough for the gas to get there, then it will ignite the whole unit. That gas coming in is passion, and once that passion ignites, now you've got a stove you can cook on, you got hot water, or whatever, and it will continue to burn until you turn it off. So you use the excitement to ignite the passion, and once that's lit, just hang on! But then you've got to take it further. You've got to take it to action. You have to go from studying, researching, identifying of the project, and convert all of that into an action plan, or else it's a waste of time. That conversion part is where people drop it.

Scott: How does purpose help you maintain that action? Even when you go, "Wow, this is tough?"

Gary: I believe, Scott, just from my experience it comes back to self-worth. If you don't know who you are and you don't have a strong ideal about who you are and what you can do, that's when you'll cave when people start telling you it's crazy or you can't do it. When you start that action plan, nothing ever goes as it was planned, and in many cases it will go almost the opposite way as if the universe is telling you, "Okay, you wanna try this? Well take it on, but you're gonna find out it's not all that great." For me, the tougher it got, the more determined I got. Instead of looking at it and saying, "Ah, geez, I can't do this," I'd look at and say, "Watch, watch." Because to me I took it as a challenge, almost a personal challenge that I can do this.

Another part for me that really helps drive me is that, I say to myself, "If God didn't want me to do this, He wouldn't have put it in my path, and if it wasn't good, it would disintegrate quickly." It's kind of like having a dream. You go to bed, you go to sleep, you have a dream, and you get all excited about whatever the dream is, and you wake up the next morning, and you can't even remember the dang dream! All you remember is being excited about it. Or, you'll go to bed and you'll have a dream, and you'll wake up the next morning, and you write the dream down because it was so real, it was so vivid, so colorful, so action-packed, and it felt so real that you never forgot one tiny piece of it. And then you started telling your friends, your wife, your spouse, whatever. When that happens, I don't look at it as a dream. To me, that's a vision, and there is a big difference. So I've learned over the years, when I wake up having a dream and it's still with me at that same intensity, then it's real, and I need to build on it.

Scott: So let's say, as we go through life, many of us when we're younger, we may not know what it is we want, that piece of being able to identify that. For some of us, we get married, we have kids. Life happens, right? If you had to think about this question, how do you determine whether you need to go after a dream or whether you need to take care of what needs to be taken care of now in this immediate future and go after your dream later? What does that look like?

Gary: This is interesting because when you're in a marriage, it's not all about you all of a sudden. When you go to your spouse and say, "You know, I have this idea, I'd really like to pursue it," and you might get the response back, "Well, do you really think at this stage in our life where we're just starting a family you should be quitting your 9-to-5 job and starting your own business?" That is a very typical response from a spouse. Our responsibility is if we feel this dream really has value, because there are a lot of dreams that don't, but if we feel this dream has value and we've studied it, you need to talk to your spouse.

Even today when I have a dream about something that I want to do, let's say it's dog racing. I talked it over with Mary, and she just absolutely, you know, knew that I'd lost it. "At your age, with the problems you've had, why would you wanna go to a place where it's forty below and race dogs in Alaska? That is insanity!" But I sit down and I talk to her, and I just let her air her feelings. Now the thing of it is, Mary didn't say you shouldn't do it or you can't do it. She is very clever. She would say there's other things you could be doing of more value. So she knows how to plant that little guilt in there that causes me to question, and feel our responsibility to our family.

If we have a dream, it's not about postponing the dream because it may never come again. Life is a window of opportunities, and when one window closes, another one will open. But it doesn't mean it's going to be a better window, and at the same time, it could be. I believe that when a door opens, it opens for the purpose of walking through it because you're going to explore another world, and there will be more doors behind that one, but our responsibility is to sit down with our family and sell them on the idea of the dream so they're in unison, so they're in harmony and supporting it. In working out the plan, you have to say, "Okay, I got this idea, and I really wanna do it. I just feel so much passion about it, but how can we do it in our lifestyle that we have today?" Mary calls it reality. Looking at that part of reality that I don't believe in, but finding the balance of where you can pursue your dream without putting it aside, but also pursue it at a pace that will have a good outcome for everybody involved.

Scott: So at the end of the day, you're winning because you're pursuing your dream, but your family is still winning because you're not putting the family at risk, or putting them in harm's way financially, emotionally, or physically to achieve something that you want. You're not being selfish with your dream.

Gary: Exactly. So it's all about synchronization, timing, and harmony. Because if your family is not in support of what you're doing, then the opposition will start to diminish your passion.

Scott: Gary, if you had anything else, any other kind of advice to give men in manning up in business, what would that be? This is your time, your floor to say, "Men, here's what you need to be doin'."

Gary: The number one greatest thing that any person can do, man or woman, is spend time getting to know who you are and developing yourself because that is your greatest investment—investing in yourself. With that, it develops your self-worth, it develops your character, it develops your commitment. If you're going to man up to anything, even if it's just building a Young Living business, it takes commitment, it takes dedication, and it takes time. Along that process, there are a lot of people saying, "You're crazy." Scott, I'll bet when you sold your chiropractic practice there were people saying, "Have you lost your flippin' mind?"

Scott: Yep!

Gary: You know, what are you going to do now? All kinds of things are said. But gentlemen, the best thing you can do is invest in yourself, trust in yourself, and live your dream.

Scott: I honestly can't put any better advice out there. This is the business section, but if you do that one thing alone, you'll see it affect other areas. All of life overlaps. If you can do that piece of advice right there, investing in yourself, figuring out who you are, moving forward with yourself, the rest of it falls into place.

Gary: Well, and the key to that for me, along with that, when we're young and we get passionate about things, we don't always think of other people, and we outpace ourselves. We move ahead of our spouse, we move ahead of our children. That becomes a very big detriment, so part of that counsel would just be to always keep in mind who is around you. As I said earlier, it's our responsibility to sell them on the idea, so that they can support it. They may not necessarily agree. Like Mary didn't agree with me going and running the dogs in Alaska at forty below, but she supported me.

Scott: And she understood you.

Gary: Yeah, she supported me, and she understood because I took time to talk to her about it. It's like I said, "Come to Alaska with me and just see. And yeah, I know it's not your thing because you like eighty degrees, not eighty below," but, you know, we're all different. The value is that I brought her along so she was part of the journey, part of the equation, and when I decided to build out the kennel here at the ranch, I sat down with her and shared with her my plans, my ideas. And the thing that's really fun is when they start giving you ideas. Then you know you've won, and I laugh about it and I tease her a lot. In fact, when Jared got married, he asked me, "Gary, if you could give me some advice as a young married man, what would it be," and I said, "Always let it be your wife's idea."

Scott: Yep, sage advice. Sage advice. That's exactly it.

Gary: So it is. I mean, anything that has value has that value to bring your loved ones with you. And guys, if you're out there building your Young Living business or your wife is and you're the support person, you know, there's not a place on earth where you can go and create what you can in Young Living and do it as a family together.

Scott: 100 percent!

Gary: It's win-win.

Scott: It is.

Gary: But take 'em for the journey.

Scott: Tell you what, thank you, Gary, I appreciate it so much, brother. I mean, to have the ability to sit down and talk with you and to get input and insight into what that looks like. My whole goal in life is to learn from people who have been there, who've done it, and who have made the mistakes already so that I hopefully make fewer. Now I'll make some, I know that. I'm not perfect, I appreciate it, so thank you.

Gary: Absolutely, Scott. You know, that's another big part of it. You can't be afraid of making a mistake. And that was something that I looked at years ago, and I thought, "Okay, I'm gonna change the dang vocabulary. It's not a mistake. I could have made a higher choice. But with the limited information I had, I made the choice to do this. If I would have had more information, I would have made a different choice. If we move away from the idea of making a mistake, emotionally, psychologically it's much more empowering to us. Because the minute we make one, we say, "Oh, geez, I made a mistake," then that's an inferiority. We're inferior because we made a mistake. It's all about seeing things as learning lessons, not making mistakes.

CHAPTER 3

MAN UP IN YOUR HEALTH

As we transition into adulthood and begin to realize the number of things that compete for our time and attention, we start lying to ourselves. We don't call it lying, we call it rationalizing. We look at our plate of life and rationalize and make excuses for why we don't have time to eat right or hit the gym. "I worked hard all day...I've got things that need to be done at home...I need to spend time with my kids...My favorite TV show is on...It's below zero outside...It's too hot to leave the house...I don't know how to use the equipment at the gym...I don't have enough money for a gym membership...I'm intimidated by others at the gym...I have an old football injury." Have I missed any?

What's your rationalization? You do realize, at the end of the day, it's simply an excuse. The value you have placed on working out and taking care of yourself is lower than the value of your excuse. Do you want to know how I know that? If you truly valued your health, you wouldn't be able to identify with any of those excuses or thought of one that wasn't listed. Trust me, if I've used one I've used them all. The problem is that excuses get easier to default to each time you use them.

Four years ago, I was T-boned by another snowmobile at eighty miles an hour and ended up, among other things, breaking five ribs. Even after the healing process, do you think it wasn't easier to say, "Man, I'm sore today, I'm going to just stay home," than to MAN UP and fight through the soreness at the gym? One year later, getting ready to move, I ripped one end of my right bicep muscle clean off the bone. Let the excuses roll, right? Nope, I committed to continue working out the rest of my body while rehabbing the bicep reattachment. Did it suck? Every single day was a battle. The following year, skydiving, I broke ribs again on the other side. There is a reason my trainer jokingly gave me the nickname "Glassman."

Running a business, spending time with our three boys, cutting enough wood to heat the house and shop during the winter, plus pursuing my many outdoor passions keep my schedule full and tend to make it difficult for me to find time to take care of myself. Does this type of day packed with things needing to be done sound familiar? Time pulls at you, responsibilities pull at you—heck, life pulls at you. I get it. These are not things that you only want and like to do, they are responsibilities that require your full-on attention.

So how do some manage it better than others? We all have the same twenty-four hours in a day, right? The difference is how we fill those twenty-four hours. A year and a half ago, after the second rib incident, I made a commitment to be healthier and get into better shape than I was twenty-plus years ago, when I got married. I looked at everything I needed and wanted to get done on my life list, outside of my fitness/health goals. Then, I looked at the time left in any given day. It didn't take long to realize I was out of time. However, I wasn't going to let that stop me. The value I placed on my goal was higher than not achieving it. I knew that if I cut out some "relaxation" time at night and went to bed a little earlier, I could get up by 4:00 a.m., get to the gym, get a good workout in, and be home in time to help get the kids up and ready for school.

Is it easy waking up at 4:00 a.m. and getting out of a warm bed, next to a warm wife, and trudging through a cold Minnesota winter morning to get my butt kicked by my trainer at 5:00 a.m.? H to the E to the double L *no*! Everything about the whole process sucks! But, when I'm done and on my way home, I have yet to feel anything but pure elation. I didn't cave to an excuse that wanted to knock another day out.

As men, why is it that we take ownership of things like our trucks, motorcycles, big boy toys, and other "stuff," yet we hand ownership over to our wives to make our doctor appointments, hand out our medication or supplements, or tell us where our stuff is? Why is it so difficult to take ownership of our own health? We need to stop waiting for or expecting someone else to make it important to us. If you're not willing to MAN UP in your health, just go ahead and say to you wife, "Here are my testicles, honey, I really don't think I need them anymore."

In the late 1990s, I learned this lesson the hard way. I used to race dirt track with my neighbor. One late night, as we were trying to fix the car for a race the next day, I ran home to get a bite to eat. Brenda asked how I was doing. I told her, "Fine, but I think I might be coming down with something 'cause I'm kinda chilly." The temperature outside was in the mid-forties, so I shouldn't have been cold. She told me, "I've got something that will warm you up." I have since learned, anything said with that particular grin she had on her face in that moment is cause for concern. She handed me six little pills and I went back over to keep working.

Within half an hour I was pouring out sweat, my T-shirt was soaked, and I felt half stoned. It wasn't until I got back home that I found out she had given me African chickweed cayenne pepper pills. Each of those bad boys were 150,000 BTU heat unit's worth of soul-scorching craziness! I made up my mind, right there and then, that I would start taking control of my own body and my own health. To this day, we laugh about it and I am grateful for her playing that little practical joke on me.

As little boys, it was okay to wait for our mommies to bring us our medicine and take care of our every need. How long has it been since you moved out of your mom and dad's house? At the end of the day, owning our health as men isn't about looking like some buff pool boy or a Chippendales dancer; it's about integrity and holding a commitment to ourselves. MAN UP and stop waiting for someone else to take ownership of your crap.

In this day and age, if you are not aware of the benefits that regular exercise can have on blood pressure, stress levels, stroke risk, and weight management, you have built one heck of a home for yourself under that rock. Plain and simple, the only answer is you have placed a much higher value on looking and feeling like crap than you have on being fit enough to play with your kids and model for them what a man taking ownership of his health looks like. We have all seen the videos on YouTube of men who could barely walk or literally couldn't fit through a door because they had let themselves go. And yet somehow, they are now incredibly active, physical specimens. What did they do? How did they do it? Honestly, there is no secret or magic pill. They simply quit making excuses and their output of calories/energy was greater than their input. Literally, that is the secret and all it really takes.

Was it easy for them? I would bet my yearly income that each and every one of them would tell you that every single day was work and a challenge! What's the difference between them and you if you are struggling with this right now? They took ownership and made correct, small, seemingly insignificant decisions each day, over a period of time. The best part of this...you can too, but only if the value you place on this decision is high enough.

Here are some strategies and motivations to help you MAN UP in your health...

Gym Bros and Brahs

Accountability in this area is absolutely needed. At the very least you need someone as a workout partner or at a minimum as an accountability partner. Preferably someone who is stronger than you in this area. It is much easier to allow yourself to be talked out of something, especially when you are the only one talking. Without having my brother-in-law Trevor holding me accountable, I can tell you without hesitation, I never would have been at the gym by 4:45 a.m.

Go Mental

If you were to talk with any elite athlete, I guarantee every single one of them would tell you how integral the mental game is to their success. To get to a professional level of excellence, mentally you have to push past the desire to quit and have the desire to push just a little bit harder than you did yesterday. Can you imagine where you would be if you used even just half the mental toughness a professional athlete does? Up your mental game...the minute you face the decision to work out or not, to eat something you know you shouldn't or not, or to slack off and do "just enough" at the gym, pause for a second, count down from five to clear those thoughts from your head, and just do the right thing. Don't give yourself time to stop or reason yourself out of it. I use this technique each morning when a reason to not work out pops into my head. "I didn't sleep very well last night...I should just sleep a little longer... 5, 4, 3, 2, 1...GET UP!"

This mental training has overlapping effect in all areas of your life. By training your mind to push past your own objections in this area, you will find it easier to push past objections or weakness in the other areas of your life as well. You will find yourself taking action faster and seeing results faster when you tune out your own excuses.

Change Your Story

Let's look first at your beliefs. What are you telling yourself when it comes to changing your health habits? Remember the list of excuses in the intro to this chapter? Not enough time, too busy, lack of knowledge, no money, injury, and so on...all of these are simply our beliefs or our triggers to rationalize our way out of doing something. You believe money is your limiting factor, when in reality my trainer has proven to me, with simple exercises using only my body weight, that he can have me crying uncle in a matter of minutes! It's free to work out at home with your own body as resistance! You might believe you are too busy to fit it into your schedule. Yet, we all find a way to fit things into our schedule that we really want to do…e.g., snowmobile trips, fishing trips, our favorite TV shows, eating out, social media, video games…need I go on? You might say, "I've had too many injuries." Okay stop, that's merely an excuse and you know it. I've had four knee surgeries, dislocated both of my shoulders more times than I can count, beat the crap out of my wrists, elbows, and shoulder while adjusting patients, torn ligaments in my ankles, and the list goes on. Unless you have been in an accident and are paralyzed from the neck down, there is always something you can do!

Think of the word "because." By simply using this word in a specific way it can change your habits. Use "because" to attach value to why you are doing it. I go to bed earlier now *because* I want to show my boys that their dad takes the time to take care of himself. I want to set the example for them to take care of themselves so they can be their best too! I watch what I eat *because* I want to look down and be able to see my shoes! And I don't want to be in the hospital with some sort of lifestyle-related disease by the time I'm fifty. I push myself at the gym *because* I want to look good for my wife and I want to be able to play and run with my kids for longer than twenty seconds without losing my breath. I also want to be around to see my boys become adults and start families of their own.

The stories we tell ourselves guide our decisions and behaviors. You are the only one who has power over these stories inside of you. As you change these stories your mind becomes better at it. No different than challenging your body, challenging your mind gets easier with practice. Change your stories…change your habits.

Stand and Deliver

Let's face it: for whatever reason, guys tend to tie being able to perform in the bedroom to their level of manliness. As we age, the degree to which our "soldier" stands at attention can change. If you want a powerful "because" like we just finished discussing, this is it!

A recent study, published in the *Journal of Sexual Medicine* looked at nearly three hundred study participants self-reporting their physical activity levels which researchers then categorized as sedentary, mildly active, moderately active, or highly active. The subjects also self-reported their sexual function, including the ability to have erections, orgasms, the quality and frequency of erections, and overall sexual function. Results found that men who reported more frequent exercise had higher sexual function scores, regardless of race. "More frequent exercise" was defined as a total of eighteen metabolic equivalents, or METS, per week. MET hours reflect both the total time of exercise and the intensity of exercise. A total of eighteen METS can be achieved by combining exercises with different intensities but is the equivalent of two hours of strenuous exercise, such as running or swimming, three and a half hours of moderate exercise, or six hours of light exercise. Long story short (I know, probably could have picked a better phrase there), regular exercise has a direct benefit for us, and our wives, in the bedroom. (You can thank you me by sharing this book with someone!)

Get Started!

One thing that pisses me off to no end is being in the gym and hearing someone belittle or laugh at someone else who is smaller or bigger than they are. I won't stand for it, and I will call out every meathead or twig that I hear doing it! By the time I'm done, they usually leave the gym with their head held low in embarrassment.

Don't do this! We all start somewhere. The guy benching three hundred pounds never started there. The gazelle on the treadmill didn't start out running five-minute miles for twenty minutes. Starting somewhere, anywhere, is the key. There are only two mistakes you can make when going after your health goals: not going all the way or not starting. Get started, follow through, and don't criticize others along the way!

Don't Just Survive...Thrive

When it comes to life, you have two choices. You can either plod through it hoping to get to tomorrow or you can thrive, taking advantage of every opportunity that presents itself because you have the energy and vitality ready and waiting.

One of my favorite things to do is hunt. If I didn't keep myself in shape and ready, I could potentially miss out, or at the very least not enjoy my time outdoors because I was too busy sucking wind. A few years ago, I got the opportunity for a mule deer hunt out west. Lucky for me, I had already begun the process of getting back into decent shape. Being a flatlander from Minnesota, there is only so much training you can do to be ready for higher elevations. Had I not already been working on staying fit, would I have gone? Of course I would have, I'm a guy! But, I know without a doubt I would have missed experiencing what I did because I would have been struggling to keep up.

When my boys ask me to ride bikes or go for a hike in the woods, my first thought is not "How am I feeling today?" or "I hope they don't want to go too far." My thought is, "Sweet! Let's go, boys!" Opportunities will come and go. The only question is: Are you ready to MAN UP in your health so when they show up, you can take advantage of them?

Pill Poppin' and Weight Droppin'

Taking ownership of your health doesn't have to mean handfuls of supplements every day or spending four hours a day, seven days a week at the gym. Unless, you have goals that require that amount of work and have that kind of time in your schedule, it simply means taking the time to invest in yourself so you can show up in life as the best you can be. There is an old saying: "You can't give what you don't have." If you lack energy or health, there is no way you can invest your energy into your wife, kids, family, or friends.

When our first son was born, everything was great until about month three. Out of the blue, he began to scratch like a dog with a bad case of fleas. It kept getting worse no matter how many doctor visits, natural therapies, or diet changes we tried. We flew him all over the country. Trust me, when I say we tried everything, we tried everything! It got so bad that his body was covered in scabs!

Eventually we found out it was eczema, which they call the "itch that rashes." We tried clipping his fingernails shorter but he flipped his hands over and figured out a way to keep scratching no matter how short his nails were. We tried socks on his hands and he figured out if he rubbed hard and fast enough, it would soothe the itch. How bad did it itch? He would itch until his skin was a bloody mess. Sleeping? That's funny. The only way he could sleep was with a nuk (pacifier) in his mouth, with me holding his hands down, head on my shoulder, bouncing and walking around the house. I would start walking with him around 9:30 p.m. and keep walking until four or so in the morning. When we sold the house, we had to replace the carpet because you could see my nightly trail in the wrecked carpet! At 4:00 a.m., I would wake Brenda and hand him off to her so I could get a couple quick hours of sleep. Then it was back up at six to get ready and head into the clinic to see patients all day. This went on for over two years before we sold the house and moved. (Coincidently, his eczema cleared up after we moved.) I say this because I was surviving. I had nothing left to give, to anyone. Exercise? That was what I did walking around the house all night. Time for myself? That was the two hours of sleep I got each night.

Granted this was extreme, and it took me a long time to get *my* health back. It wasn't all in one month, one year, or even two years. But, I now maintain that health, so I am capable of giving back and pouring into others who need me. There was nothing extreme that I did to get my health back, nor to maintain my health. Do I take supplements and go to the gym? Yep, I sure do! But it's not handfuls, and I certainly don't spend four hours a day at the gym. Are there days when I miss a workout because of travel or a commitment that can't be changed? Of course I do, I'm human just like you. However, I make sure I make it up somehow. It may be a bike ride later with the kids, or a walk with my wife, or burpees, push-ups, and sit-ups in the shop or at my hotel when I travel. The value I place on my health is high enough and my habit is strong enough that I won't allow myself to miss out.

You may not know this but my undergraduate degree is in exercise physiology (working out), yet I still pay a trainer to kick my butt once a week and make sure I am doing things right without cheating. There is a reason for that...typically someone else will push us harder than we push ourselves and hold us to a higher standard. This is the reason I picked Aaron Bemboom to interview for this chapter.

MAN UP in Your Health: Interview with Aaron Bemboom

Scott: What is your background and education, Aaron?

Aaron: I have my associate of arts degree from St. Cloud State, my health and exercise science degree from Minnesota School of Business, and I am a certified National Strength and Conditioning Association personal trainer.

Scott: If I were to say that you are the expert in manning up for fitness and health, what does that mean to you?

Aaron: I think manning up in fitness and health is doing it even though you don't want to, being faithful and consistent. You're going to have mornings that you don't want to do it or days you don't want to do it or excuses that come up. In health and exercise you have to be faithful, and the definition of faithful is to be persistent or showing up every day, being unfailingly loyal and consistent regardless of extenuating circumstances. So no matter what else you have going on that day, you're still going to get that workout in.

Scott: So you're saying that people have excuses.

Aaron: People have excuses, and I haven't heard of a good one yet.

Scott: Have you heard the same ones multiple times?

Aaron: Oh, tons. You get the same thing. "Billy's got this...Sammy's got that." A lot of it is blamed on family. Unfortunately, people don't realize by working out and exercising you're helping your family. You become a bigger blessing to them by being a healthier and more active person.

Scott: Let's explore that a little bit. How does you working out and becoming healthy bless your family more than if you wouldn't work out?

Aaron: Family-wise, going small picture, I am able to be active with my wife and my children. My sons are involved in activities, my daughter is involved in activities, and because I am physically fit, it's easier for me to be active with them. I am able to be a coach in their activities, like baseball, something I'm not an expert in, but I can do it. Wrestling, I am an expert at wrestling, and I am able to be a part of their lives in teaching them how to be better wrestlers, by being active and on the mat with them.

Looking at the bigger picture, like family and friends, I always joke that God put me on this earth to move things. I get called probably once a week to move something big and heavy that someone else doesn't want to move. Whether it is putting a dock in, taking a dock out, moving a dresser or moving a person. Everyone has a family member that's got a friend that has a friend needing something moved. In the case of my family the response is, "Call Aaron. He's strong and he'll come do it." So that is how it has affected probably my friends and family, they can rely on me for things like that.

Scott: You said you've got two boys and a daughter, correct?

Aaron: Yes.

Scott: What are their ages?

Aaron: Owen is eight, Everett is six, and Rosie just turned four.

Scott: So obviously, you want to lead that example for all of those kids because they're important to you, all of them. Does it look any different for you when you look at your boys versus Rosie?

Aaron: Yeah. I want them to know that it's not easy. Life doesn't just hand you everything, and like I've said multiple times, sometimes you have to embrace the suck. You have to do the hard things in life. It's not all sunshine and rainbows. You're going to have hard days, you're going to have bad days, and guess what? Being in shape makes those times easier. You know, if I'm not battling heart disease or high blood pressure or diabetes, and I'm having a bad day, I can look around and be like, "You know what? Life's not that bad. I don't have cancer, I don't have these other extenuating circumstances." It goes beyond just teaching the boys that being healthy and being active is important; I make sure they see it every day. Dad gets up early every day and he stays late at work every day. They also see how I'm burning the candle at both ends, but I still make time for them. Because staying fit is a priority, I still have the energy to go play ball with them in the yard, go play catch with the football or go to wrestling practice and not just sit on the sideline and be a wrestling dad that way, but be actively teaching them. I'm in there doing the conditioning with them and I think that's something unique.

Scott: We talked a little about the importance for your boys, what about the importance for your daughter? When it comes to her, what is the importance of her seeing you being physically fit, healthy, and in shape for her as a girl growing up?

Aaron: That she can do it too, that she doesn't have to be on the sideline. She can be healthy and active, she can do things, she can be strong, she can be physically fit and do whatever she wants. She doesn't have to be asking for help. And it goes beyond fitness. It goes into any activity of life. She is going to know how to change her own oil. She is going to know how to change her car tire. She is going to be able to do those things for herself. She is not going to need to depend on people, but even looking further into the future, like her dating or looking for a spouse, I want her to find a companion who is physically active and fit and will be able to protect her and provide and be another rock in her life, bring strength.

Scott: Does your wife lay out your vitamins or medications for you?

Aaron: Not once. Never.

Scott: One of the epiphanies I talk about in the book was when Brenda gave me six African chickweed, 150,000 BTUs each, cayenne pepper pills. From that point forward, I never let her lay another thing out for me. But I look at this whole manning up piece, and it's like, okay, we take ownership of all this crap in our lives and toys and trucks and cars and houses and jobs, but so many men don't take ownership of their own health. It's like oh, my wife's got to make my doctor's appointment, my wife's got to lay out all my pills, whether it's supplements or medications. Do you feel that men need to man up in that area?

Aaron: Yeah, they need to. It is your life. You need to be responsible and held accountable for your actions. If you're too much of a lazy idiot to lay out your own pills, then you can suffer the consequences. I have been saying it for years: we need to take warning labels off of things and let natural selection take its course. It's ridiculous the things warning labels are on. If you don't understand that hot coffee will burn you, then don't order hot coffee.

Scott: I think too, if guys could have just a simple win there, it's all about small successes and winning, getting one win under your belt and moving to the next one. That's one of my biggest pet peeves. When I see guys and they say, "My wife's going to make me an appointment," my first thought is, what the _____?

Aaron: You don't know how to operate your phone? You don't know your schedule?

Scott: Now, I know your schedule, and I know your schedule is just absolutely nuts. You also are in training for a show, and what's the show called?

Aaron: It is going to be a classic physique competition.

Scott: You also coach wrestling.

Aaron: Yes.

Scott: You are a husband, so you need to spend some time with your wife as well.

Aaron: Yes.

Scott: I'm sure many ask how you are able to do all this.

Aaron: Like I said before, burning the candle on both ends, you have to have the ability to be a morning person. I start every day at four thirty if not earlier, and it is about having that energy. I have to bring it every day. I can't have a bad day at a class or with a client. They don't care. I need to bring energy and excitement to that training session every time, and if I wasn't in shape, I wouldn't have the energy to do that. If I wasn't in shape, I wouldn't be able to be a coach for my sons. If I wasn't in shape, I wouldn't have any clients. I'm a walking billboard, I am my own business card. If I'm in a T-shirt or if I'm in shorts or if I'm in a tank top and my arms don't look good, that's on me. I need to be in shape. The cool thing is, by being in shape it allows me to have the energy and drive to do all of those things and more.

Scott: What are the top three wrong things people do when they go back to the gym or start for the first time?

Aaron: When they first start, they don't ask for help. So ask for help! Even if it's the manager that signs you up, another gym member, at least they have some knowledge, but the biggest thing is find a trainer. Find a trainer at your gym. I guarantee your gym has a trainer. Ask them: "How do I do this? How do I use that? What should I be doing?" Pay the money. By and large, you will get more out of that one session with him and just getting a little bit of knowledge and keeping yourself safe than the thousands of doctor bills you will have from wrecking your back by doing something wrong.

Scott: So you're saying you see quite a few people that come into the gym and do it absolutely bassackwards?

Aaron: Exactly. Right! That's probably the biggest mistake people do. Number two, going too hard too fast. I equate working out in fitness to swimming. You don't dive off the high board into the deep end the first day of swimming lessons. You play in the kiddie pool for a while, right? Learn how your body reacts to different exercises or different times of day that you are working out or different workouts if nothing else. Some people can lift weights no problem, and if they do a cardio session, they will be puking in a bucket. Some people can handle cardio like nothing, and if they get a resistance training session with me, they will throw up. Go easy, take it slow, ask advice.

The biggest problem is people quit. Don't quit. Fitness is not instant gratification. It is not. It is a process. It is a journey. What I am doing today, I will not see results from that for months. It takes time. Yeah, I could bust my butt this week and I could lose five pounds, great, I will feel better about myself. But in the long run, my heart will be better, my muscles are stronger, and my joints are better. That's a long-haul process. That's not what I'm doing. What I do today, I won't see in three days, but I might see it in three months, three years, or in thirty years, and that's the long haul. Stay patient and work through the process.

Scott: What is your biggest hurdle in fitness and in health?

Aaron: My biggest hurdle in fitness and health, I love food. Food and me are best friends, and I wish it was just the healthy food, but I really enjoy dessert. I really enjoy a good steak, which in moderation, fine, have it. I'm a bottomless pit. I will eat until I darn near throw up, and then once I throw up, I will come back for seconds. I always tell people that working out and exercising, that's the easy part. Diet and nutrition is the hard part. Unfortunately, 60 percent, 70 percent of where you're going to see your results is what you put in your mouth, and guess what? You only have one person to blame for that. You're not tied to the table. You're not forced to eat what you're eating. You make conscious decisions on what choices you make.

Scott: I know how important this is to me and what I feel about it, but when you see people coming into the gym or starting to work out or trying to lose weight, how big of a piece does and should the accountability factor play?

Aaron: Huge because guess what? Losing weight and exercising is hard, and no one does anything hard for themselves. You need somebody else to hold you accountable to be like, "Hey, I'm gonna be there at six o'clock. I'm gonna be there working out. I want you to be there. We're going to be there together. We're going to do this together." So finding a person, a partner to hold you accountable and check you when you miss. What is your excuse? Why weren't you here? You better have a good one. And if you weren't here this morning, you better be there tonight, and you know what? Send me a picture of your workout. Tag me in your workout. Tell me what you did. Give me a call. Ask me questions, like what did you do this morning. What did I do? It's so huge to have, and not just one person. I wouldn't just have one accountability partner. You got to have five or six or seven or eight or a hundred people that are saying hey, did you do what you were supposed to do today? Did you go to the gym? Did you eat what you were supposed to eat today? Otherwise, you don't do hard things for yourself. You do hard things for other people.

Scott: One last question for you because one of the biggest things we hear, and I'm sure you've heard it, and I've heard it many, many times, is I can't afford to go to a gym.

Aaron: Plain and simple that is a bull crap excuse.

Scott: So, what can you really do on a limited budget?

Aaron: Even if you take a gym out of it, you have arms and legs, right? I know it's Minnesota, but you can go for a run. You can go for a walk. You can find a hill, walk the hill. Drop down and do some push-ups. Even if they're modified. If you have got a hard PT session and you can't do twelve push-ups, it happens, but you should be able to start out somewhere. You squat down every time you're sitting at the dinner table, or you sit down on the couch and you have to stand back up, right? Guess what...you're doing squats. So you're watching TV, a commercial comes on, drop down, do twenty squats, do fifteen push-ups. I don't know if you noticed that, but that won't cost you anything but time.

Scott: I've been through training sessions before with you where there have been no weights involved. It's body weight, and within minutes, I'm crying for my mommy.

Aaron: Yeah, I can absolutely destroy people by using their own body. I have done hour-long classes where we have not touched a weight, and you will feel miserable at the end of it, I guarantee it.

Scott: So you're saying if somebody really says, "You know what, I really want to get in shape, I'm committed, I don't necessarily have the money for a gym membership right now, but I could pay a trainer to give me a list of things that I could be doing at home," a home workout with no weights involved that could get them back on track to becoming in shape?

Aaron: Absolutely.

Scott: So there are no excuses really that are valid?

Aaron: Money plays no role in health because it does not cost you anything to move. And food-wise, people, well, they say health food is so expensive. No, it's not. It's not. If you do it the way you're supposed to and you look at the calories you're going to get from something healthy versus the calories you're going to get from crap, eat the good stuff. It's not more expensive. It's not.

Scott: It's just whether or not people see the value in the time it takes to do it.

Aaron: If you're really worried about a buck, the food you put into you, you let me know what your doctor bills cost for diabetes and your medication costs. I will save you thousands and thousands of dollars in medical bills if you join a gym.

Scott: One of my favorite comments I've heard, and I used to use it when I was practicing, was if you're saving up for a rainy day, guess what, it's pouring out. One of the best investments you can make is in yourself, whether personal development or physical development, investing back in yourself.

Aaron: Absolutely. I tell clients they are no good to their family dead. That is my motivation for some people, because that's what they need to hear. You are killing yourself every day you make bad decisions, whether it's not exercising, smoking, drinking, or the food choices you make. I know everyone's got family or friends that love them and want them to be around. Make a decision to be around. I know it sucks and working out is not everyone's cup of tea. Eating healthy is not everyone's bundle of fun either, but being there for your daughter's graduation or your son's wedding or your granddaughter's birth or your retirement is the bundle of fun you want to be around for. How about enjoying that retirement? How many people do you know that retire and die within a year? You've worked your whole life thinking "I don't have time to work out." You keep working and working and working and working, and you get to the point where you can enjoy life, then you die because you didn't take care of yourself. That's a kick in the nuts if anything. That's why guys like you and I do what we do. We invest in ourselves and our health. You are no good to anyone dead.

CHAPTER 4

MAN UP AS A FRIEND

Have you ever gone out with your buddies, whether golfing, hunting, or playing cards, to come home to the age-old question: "What did you guys talk about?" And, have you ever answered, "Not much, guy stuff," or, "Nothing really." Why is it that as kids we talk about everything under the sun, but as we progress into adulthood, the topics of conversation for men become superficial at best? Think for a second about what you used to talk about with your buddies in grade school, middle school, and high school. We all talked about our dreams of becoming a professional athlete, rock star, or race car driver, and the list goes on. Or we talked about girls, and what it would be like to kiss a girl, get married, and have sex (yeah you know you did, don't try to deny it).

The point is, we were curious, and we talked with each other about these things because none of us ever thought we "shouldn't." So why is it, that as most men age, these types of conversations and our openness shut down? Is it because we became lazy and let go of our dreams as we were forced to meet the "reality" of the real world? Is it because we were made fun of for being open or too sensitive? Or, is it because we started comparing ourselves to other men, based on the little information we could see from a distance, and developed a story in our heads about how successful they are and how they "have it all together" where we don't? These are the stories that keep us from being real about the struggles we all have with our work, wives, kids, and even our faith.

Are we just that scared that someone is going to see through the thin veil of protection that we all hide behind, in a poor attempt to portray that we somehow have it all together and have life by the balls? Are we afraid that someone is going to get a glimpse of who and what we're really like?

If you are a parent, I want you to think about a time when you were invited over to someone else's house. We've all been there...we talk to the kids *before getting in the car*, telling them how we expect them to behave so much differently than what they normally do at home. We talk to them *in the car* on the way there, reminding them to be on their best behavior, and maybe even try to bribe or threaten them with taking something away if they misbehave. Of course, when we arrive, we remind them again *just before getting out of the car* as well. Then it happens...the other couple's kids do something inappropriate and yours don't. There is that moment of silent inward celebration, the kind where if you weren't within view of the other parents, you might actually jump in the air and do a fist pump, that it finally wasn't your kids this time! Don't deny it, you feel a little guilty...but not that guilty. Later that night you and your wife are talking about the evening and you both breathe a sigh of relief. You talk about how great it is that it's not "just you" and maybe you are not such bad parents after all.

In reality this is no different than what we do as men. We analyze our own actions silently, often painfully, and in the rare occurrence a fellow man slips and reveals some sort of inadequacy, instead of rallying alongside him and letting him know he is not alone, we inwardly pump our fists and jump for joy that someone else is as infallible as we are. Oftentimes, being alone in our heads like that is no different than a prison sentence of solitary confinement. At least if you're among other men with a "gen-pop" prison sentence, you have the ability to talk to others and see that you are not the only one struggling.

Oceans of Emotions

Men have a strength that can be both reassuring and devastating. Unfortunately, it's like there is an unwritten man code that says it's okay to talk about anything except feelings, pain, or shortcomings. For some it may be a "strength" thing. It's a false notion that believes, "If I show any kind of emotion, people will see me as weak."

Believe me, I know this firsthand. I went through a good portion of my life not letting anyone—and I mean anyone—see a hint of emotion or "weakness." However, I learned through experience and pain how detrimental that was to me and to those I cared most about. I thought that as a man I was supposed to be stoic and unflappable, the fierce protector if you will. I achieved it too, but I was also unapproachable and unfeeling. The voicing of my pain came across as pain to others. I thought I was being a MAN, but I couldn't have been more wrong. I was more of a hurting child than I was living the definition of what a man should be. The extent of my conversations with other men was a grunt and a punch, and if they slipped up and showed any vulnerability, that was my "in" to take advantage of their weakness. I was stuck in that solitary confinement sentence in my own head, with no one to talk to or vent my frustrations, failures, or dreams.

The truth is, showing or expressing your emotions doesn't mean you have to cry at sunsets, or every time your wife or kids say "I love you," or when you see pictures of fluffy kittens on Facebook. It simply means being willing to completely and effectively express what's going on inside of you in your own way. It wasn't until a couple more mature men I knew spoke into my life that I even realized this. This wasn't a direct, intervention-type of thing either. It was more of an indirect observation on my part of guys expressing their frustrations, failures, and pain. Yet, the difference was they listened and encouraged one another. They didn't attack, but nor did they take the other guy's side immediately either. If there was an action or mentality needing correction, they called the guy on it, and offered to hold each other accountable moving forward. They listened to and counseled each other. Much like a marriage needs open and honest lines of communication to succeed and flourish, so do our relationships with other men. There a few things to remember when learning how to master the art of being a number one bro.

Your Wife Is Not Your Bro

A great marriage is when you are married to your best friend. However, there are some things (okay, a lot of things) that women just don't understand when it comes to how men think. Quite honestly this point goes both ways. You should not be your wife's "BFF" either. Men and women think differently, because we are different. Guys who are married and don't have much in the way of male friends tend to rely too much on their wives and expect too much from them. Having a buddy to talk to about guy stuff saves your wife from having to pretend she is interested. Likewise, her having a BFF saves you from needing to pretend like you have any interest in high-heel shoes. (Besides making sure she knows how hot she looks in them, of course!) I don't know where the idea came from that as married couples, we are to have complete interest in everything our spouse does. It's ridiculous. I would never expect my wife to pretend she has any interest whatsoever, in the progression of Harley-Davidson motors from the Flathead to the Shovelhead and on to the Milwaukee-Eight (unless that's her thing too). I know that's not her thing and she knows which interests she has that are not mine. It's okay to have different interests; in fact, it's a good thing. Some of it is likely what attracted you to her in the first place.

I've Got Your Six

The phrase "I've got your six"—meaning "I've got your back"—comes from the elite brotherhood, forged in fire, of those in our armed forces who go through hell and back. It is a tight bond that is rarely broken and rarely penetrated. A fundamental piece in any long-standing, honest, tight and healthy relationship is loyalty. We're talking the kind of loyalty where you would take a bullet for the other person. Very few of us wouldn't take one for our wife or kids. If you wouldn't, dude, you need more work and help than this book is able to provide.

Here's the thing though. If your list of people you would truly take a bullet for is longer than the list of those you wouldn't, you need to reassess your priorities and learn how to say no. The type of bro or accountability brother that you would do this for shouldn't fill a single-spaced, college-ruled piece of paper front and back. If it does, you are either spending too much time and energy on people outside of your family or you will never find a woman, because your schedule doesn't leave any time for it. This should be an elite group of men that you trust one hundred percent, where you are all committed to moving each other forward in life.

I get it, it isn't necessarily easy to find guys like this. It's also going to take showing some vulnerability around guys that you think may fit the bill. And guess what? At some point you are going to make the wrong choice and you may end up pissed off when they cut you down for opening up. That's okay—it only makes the choice clear that they do not belong in your band of brothers. Remember, if you're in your head, you're dead. We all need time out of the solitary confinement in our head to exercise in the yard. And, as men we need those close relationships with other men where the mentality is: I've been in your shoes, I know what you are going through, I have your back no matter what, but I'm not your *yes* man.

Healthy Competition

When it comes to competition, the only one you should be in true competition with and comparing yourself against is the reflection in the mirror. We've all heard it, and I covered it earlier, and we understand the concept. However, there is a form of competition with others that can serve us well. I'm talking about healthy, friendly competition between you and your elite band of brothers. In this type of competition, you don't set out to *crush* your opponent. Your goal is to help them be a better version of themselves while at the same time becoming a better version of yourself.

As men, we love competing. Why do you think there are games like H-O-R-S-E, or why the score is kept in baseball and basketball. Why do we have chips when playing poker? Every one of these is a measuring stick of sorts. The score tells us where we are in our skill. The problem starts when we inaccurately compare ourselves to an impossible standard that someone else sets.

I love to play men's slow-pitch softball during the summer, and I am always trying to get better. Belting balls out of the park is not my specialty, even though every now and then even a blind squirrel finds a nut. I am more of a single/double placement type of player. I play ball with my brother-in-law Trevor, who is a giant of a man. At six eight, three hundred–plus pounds, he is the walking definition of a power hitter. A regular-sized bat looks like a freaking toothpick in his hands!

I remember the time his dog died the day of a game. Very rarely do you see him get angry, unless someone intentionally walks him. His first hit of the game, the ball was still going up as it flew forty yards past the centerfield fence. His next at bat, as expected, they began to pitch him low. The ball was barely making it to the plate. As ball four came in, he swung the bat like a golf club and put it over the right field fence. When he came up for at bat number three, they decided to pitch him high. (At six eight, you can imagine how high the balls were coming in.) The last thing the other team wanted was a repeat of the previous two at bats. And wouldn't you guess it—ball four came in again and he swung fully stretched like a kid swinging at a piñata hung too high. This one went over the left field fence. As soon as the ball left the bat, in disgust the pitcher threw his glove in the air and walked off the field.

Do I compete with Trev in softball? Dang right I do, but I don't compare myself to his ability to hit the long ball. I am not physically built like him, but we push each other to get better. We congratulate one another when we do good and just as quickly we will harass each other when we make a mistake. We both know where it's coming from and it doesn't hurt our feelings, but onlookers don't necessarily get it. It's simply because they don't have the friendship we have with each other. No one else talks to us the way we talk to each other. That on and off the field banter actually prods us to do better. Don't buy into the talk about competition being bad; it's hardwired into us as guys. We are not designed for the "participation trophy" mentality. We are designed for an "iron sharpening iron" mentality. That is what healthy relationships and healthy competition with other men gives us.

9-Line It

Another military term, but it fits too well not to use it. The phrase "9-Line" is a military term that medevacs use for calling in a combat injury, because it is the best way to calmly and accurately report that a soldier needs medical attention. There isn't a relationship on this third rock from the sun that doesn't experience hurt, tension, or conflict. It is common sense: just as a wound on the battlefield needs as immediate attention as possible, a wound in a relationship is really no different. If left unaddressed, the wound will fester and worsen, often resulting in irreparable damage.

Whatever the reason, many guys will just try to ignore or self-treat these types of wounds, whether it is retreating to that solitary confinement cell in their head or self-medicating with alcohol, drugs, video games binges, or whatever it takes to avoid what they don't want to face. Many times, these relationship wounds aren't even intended, they are due to friendly fire. At the end of the day though, the wound still needs to be brought to light and dealt with so that healing can begin.

It may look something like this:

"Dude, what you said the other day really pissed me off."

"Sorry, man, I didn't even think about it like that."

Quick and simple…irrigate the wound, stitch it up, and move on.

Your Ego Is Not Your Amigo

In almost all areas of our lives, the biggest trap or pitfall in accomplishing a goal, improving yourself, or growing in a relationship is your ego. As men, our egos tend to be like a balloon. Our egos can be both inflated or deflated, but the way this is done is important. Just like a balloon, too much pressure too quickly can pop it. Inflation needs to be done carefully. On the flip side, like a sharp needle to a balloon, our ego can be popped instead of being deflated carefully in the event of overinflation. None of us want to admit it, but a hard shot to the ego might as well have been a sword to the heart. This type of blow from another man or a woman can be fatal to the relationship. Keeping our ego in check is something we should always be working on, but sometimes that can work out as well as asking a cat to take care of a mouse. As men, we place a high value on respect. We need the accountability piece, but we must also be careful in providing it to others as well. When we pop someone else's ego balloon, instead of walking alongside them and slowly deflating it, the respect piece is what becomes damaged.

There are three simple things we can do to keep our ego in check:

Reflect on your weaknesses. Taking time to be honest about and look at where you fail is important. You will never work on something that isn't at the front of your mind or even on your radar. Remember though—there is a fine line between agonizing over something and admitting a shortcoming to work on.

Have good friends and listen to them. This is much more than the "screen-click friendship" that is watering down what friendship should be. A real relationship between people with in-depth knowledge about and respect for each other is still crucial even in the digital world we live in today.

Accept your kudos, but don't let it go to your head. In ancient Rome, the Auriga was a slave with gladiator status. Legend has it, this was the same name given to the slave who held the laurus crown during Roman triumph parades over the head of the *dux* (leader/general). The Auriga would continuously whisper *"Memento homo"* ("Remember you are only a man") to keep all the celebration from going to the leader's head. We all need someone to be an Auriga in our lives, someone who will make sure our balloon doesn't get overinflated and pop.

If My Absence Makes No Impact, Then My Presence Is a Joke

To maintain any relationship, regular communication is needed. Years ago, if you were not close in proximity, communication meant actually sitting down and taking the time to write a letter, go to the post office, and put it in the mail. With the telephone, regular communication became much easier. Nowadays, it's a snap with Snapchat, text messaging, or Facebook. Yet even now, this incredible invention of being able to talk over a wire to someone thousands of miles away, or now with no wires, seems to be going the way of the letter. Our conversations have been shortened into bite-size little phrases of abbreviated words, shorthand acronyms like FWIW, IDK, or IOW (for what it's worth...I don't know...in other words). True communication is more than these abbreviations can accomplish. Don't believe me? Try answering all of your wife's questions for a day with only these abbreviations or short text message-style answers.

The relationships we have with other guys in our lives take real work just like any other relationship. If we aren't adding value to or our friends' lives or they aren't adding value to our life, it's time to start rethinking that friendship. Here is where I am most likely going to challenge some men's thinking. There is an age-old debate on how men communicate differently than women and how men prefer side-by-side interaction more than facing each other when communicating. It's believed that men don't need to go deep into conversations, and that their superficial talk about sports, tools, or work is really a carefully constructed way of talking about love and feelings without actually talking about it.

Sorry, I call BS. If you truly want to have a conversation about your struggles and failures or feelings, then MAN UP, find someone who will listen, and actually articulate how you feel. Here's the kicker: in order to do this, there needs to be a level of trust and respect. When you don't do something to maintain relationships with other men in your life, the chances of them being there for you and willing to listen drop dramatically. As men, we need that understanding of who we are from another man to help us through our challenges. There are some things that women just don't get about us. But, if we make no effort to impact the men in our inner circle, there will be no impact in our absence, and in fact our presence is a joke. C.S. Lewis penned: "Friendship is unnecessary, like philosophy, like art.... It has no survival value; rather it is one of those things which give value to survival."

As I write this section I can only hope for two things:

1. Those who I consider my true friends know it.
2. They know their value to my survival.

Men Aren't Women... Quit Trying to Turn Us into Them!

I have talked about how as men we need to be okay with effective communication. How we are different from women and how trying to understand them is important. But, at the end of the day, men still need to be men. Understanding our emotions is something we as men should strive for; however, becoming emotional just for the sake of being emotional goes against everything in our internal code. The last thing men want to be around is an overemotional man who cries all the time. Heck, women don't even want a man who cries more than they do either. I'm not saying it's bad if a man cries. There are going to be times in all of our lives where grief rips through you, and it's healthy to let it out.

For this chapter, the man I chose to add value to how important friendships among men are is someone who has been there for me and willing to speak truth into my life. His name is Randy Murrah, and I consider him one of my closest friends.

MAN UP as a Friend: Interview with Randy Murrah

Scott: Randy, when I say we as men need to man up in friendship, what does that mean to you?

Randy: To me, to man up in friendship means that you don't want me to blow smoke up your ass. Because a lot of times in friendships, depending on the depth that they are, I don't think that you will challenge somebody with a different view if it's not that important. So if you come to me, you say I want to man up this friendship, I want you to speak into my life whenever you see me going down a path that doesn't seem right. Then I'm going to have permission to give you my viewpoint on that.

I have a friend who I have been friends with forever, and we can discuss religion, but I don't follow his viewpoints on religion, and he doesn't necessarily follow mine. Since we're not likely to change each other's minds, I'm not looking for him to speak faith or religion, probably more so faith, into my life. We don't need to go down that path. You know, I don't need him telling me that I don't need to go to this church or believe this way or that I need to believe the way he believes. Whereas if he was to say to me, "You know, I want to man up this friendship. I want to hold you to speak truth into my life when you see me going astray." Then I would definitely speak to him about that again and keep hammering him on it until he said, "Got it, that's enough, I don't need you to do that anymore." He either changes his viewpoint or says he's had enough. So to man up is to give me permission to speak about sensitive subjects in a friendship.

Scott: So, what do you think it is that we as men are able to talk about anything and everything to each other when we are young. Yet, all of a sudden, it's like those close relationships that we had when we were kids are gone when we get into manhood. Why do you think that is?

Randy: I think that pride gets in the way. I'm doing better than you, you know, and I don't want to hurt your feelings so I'm not going to get as deep into that stuff, or you're doing better than me, and we're just not going to talk about certain things. But I think, the first thing that comes to my mind is our pride gets in the way.

Scott: How important it is for guys out there who may not be doing it right now, may not have that close friendship or that accountability type of a friendship? I mean we've all got friends, but more of that accountability type of friendship with another guy? Whether that's accountability in their marriage, their faith, as a father, whatever it is. How important has it been in your life, and is it at this point in your life?

Randy: Okay, so this can be a pretty tough question because depending on where you want to grow or what you want to become, it can be vastly important or not really important at all. There have been times in my life when I didn't really have nor did I want anybody to speak into my life. As my family was growing up, I moved around quite a bit. I didn't have a lot of close friends; in fact, I had very few close friends. I still have my one friend from childhood that I've had all my life. Even though we live hundreds or thousands of miles apart, we continue to talk to each other. We are the kind of guys that even though we hadn't seen each other for a few years, once we are together, it's like we've never been apart. However, through much of that time I didn't necessarily really want him speaking anything into my life, because nobody, including him, was close enough to qualify for that position.

But if you're someone who wants to grow and become a better person, I think it's very important for you to have friends and/or mentors that you will allow to have that position of being able to speak in your life. I have got that now with you, Steven, and Pastor Jim, but really you guys are probably the only three people I want to have speaking to me about where I need to go.

I'll also allow electronic mentors, meaning people that I follow, Andy Andrews or Eric Worre, I'll allow those people to speak into my life.

Scott: You just mentioned three people you know personally and some you know virtually who influence your life the most. What would you say is that magical number before the voices get to be too many in your head? For something like, as deep as we're talking, where somebody is speaking truth about your actions in your faith, as a father, as a husband, all that type of like, whoa, this is some serious stuff?

Randy: For me, it would probably be no more than four.

Scott: And for the guys that are out there, if I shut my eyes and think, I can think of four or five names of guys you can always see, whether it is on Facebook or something else. They're reaching out for somebody else's input into what they're doing, and they're getting fifty different answers, and I think they end up with that paralysis of analysis. They don't know where to go.

Randy: For me, I don't want to maintain that many close friendships, because I'm a fairly private person. I don't let a lot of emotion out. I just don't want that many people around me.

I mean, you ask fifty different people a question, you're going to get fifty different answers if it's a subjective question. That is too much information at once to do anyone any good.

Scott: For the guys who may not have that kind of a friend, how do they or what do they need to do to find someone who can be that type of a mentor or a friend?

Randy: Well, first, you have to choose to associate with other guys. There's always a venue for association, whether it's a church or a bar or the softball team. You need to find someplace where you're going to meet other people. You're going to want to strike up or nurture a friendship with someone whom you would want to emulate some portion of their life. You look for someone who has got it together in a certain area(s). First though, in order to get a friend, you have to be a friend, and be willing to put time and effort into building that relationship. Friendships can take a lot of time to develop, at least deep friendships do. There is trust that has to be developed, and that trust goes both directions. You can think about it and think about it and think about it all you want, but it doesn't do you a lot of good. You've got to get out and take action. You've got to get out and mix it up with real people, not just people on the computer.

Scott: You need to get a little dirty?

Randy: Get a little dirty, get some dirt under your fingernails and get into the nuts and bolts of life and have discussions. I don't think that you can determine who that mentor-type friend is going to be if you're not willing to bare a little of your soul and have some one-on-one discussions.

Scott: You talked about that, that nurturing piece and that baring of your soul. It almost sounds like there needs to be more than just a little effort on your part.

Randy: Absolutely.

Scott: So on that whole effort piece, there is a quote, and I talked about it in this chapter, "If my absence makes no impact, then my presence is a joke." When we look at that, and think about the vulnerability piece you spoke of, how do we relate that to this friendship piece among guys?

Randy: Well, it's a lot easier to be vulnerable, I think, with friends. And again, being vulnerable in front of somebody goes back to trust. "I'm going to show you this silly side of me. What are you going to do with that? Are you going to bring that back up in front of my wife to make me look stupid? If you are, I'm not going to show you that piece. Am I going to tell you some of my inner-most struggles only to have you go back and talk to the next guy down the road and say, "Well, at least you're not like ol' Randy over there who's struggling with _____." So that trust portion is paramount with a deep, binding friendship. I know that with my friendship with Mark, I could probably tell him anything, and it wouldn't go anywhere, he wouldn't hold it over my head. There is a lot of effort and time that has to be put into developing a friendship that goes that deeply.

Scott: They say that for women, the biggest thing they want to feel in the relationship is being loved and understood or listened to. For most men, it's that they want to feel respect. I think that whole piece with trust as men, it may take a while, but if we allow that trust and respect to be built, then vulnerability can happen. Without respect and trust, I just don't see vulnerability even beginning anywhere.

Randy: No. I know army buddies go a step even deeper because they're putting their life on the line for their buddy. Some of those same guys, even twenty years later, would give up their life for their buddy without thinking twice.

Scott: For those guys that's a relationship with trust and respect that's forged in a whole different kind of hell than most of us will ever go through.

Randy: Hopefully, yeah.

Scott: Do you think there's an opportunity for guys in general to forge that kind of a relationship with other guys if they are willing to do the hard work that comes with it?

Randy: If both parties are willing to work equally as hard. If one's not willing to work as hard as the other, it's going to be lopsided, and it's not going to go as deep.

Scott: So, let's talk about competition a little bit, competition amongst guys and their buddies. Bad? Good? What do you feel?

Randy: Well, I think competition among guys can be very good. It's not only good, but I think it's healthy. Especially between guys, it's typically what drives us. You always want to be able to beat your buddy at something. I think if you're a winner, the winner needs to be a gracious winner, and the loser needs to be a gracious loser. I'm sure it sucks if you're the one who always loses.

Scott: Like you said, I haven't met a buddy yet where I've been able to beat him at everything, and there's going to be something where he is going to beat me. The important thing to remember is even though there's going to be competition between each other, my main competition is with myself. I'm always trying to be better than I was yesterday or the last time I tried it. Otherwise, like you said, if you're always losing, man, it sucks. I don't want to play that game anymore. I'm going to take my ball and go home.

Randy: And competition can be fierce between buddies. I know, and I refer back to Mark a lot because we've had a lot of life experiences, but we used to play racquetball a couple of nights a week. At times, it seemed like we were trying to kill each other. Sometimes he won, sometimes I won, and, I mean, it was a battlefield on the court. However, once we left the court, we left it on the court. You have to be able to celebrate the other's successes and not be concerned with losing. Think about the paintball outings you and I have done. Somebody's going to win, and somebody's going to lose. It's fierce competition in the middle of it, but once we're done, we're done.

Scott: Everybody's having a beer and relaxing and swapping stories about…"Dude, you killed me on that one. Well, you killed me on the other one."

Randy: Exactly, it's good to have competition, but to always be able to let it go, and sadly, some friends can't let it go. I think about the movie, Rudy, and when one of his teammates said, "You play every scrimmage like it's the frickin' Super Bowl." And while we need that, I think, sometimes friendly competition doesn't need me to go all out trying to just annihilate you every time.

Scott: Right. It's like poker. When we have our poker nights. We're there. Our main reason for being there is to enjoy each other's company, tell stories, be away from the wives, and just hang out with the other guys. Now, is it fun when we just nail somebody on a hand or two? Of course it is, but that's not our main premise of being there. We're not there to take home the entire pot. We're there to have a good time.

Randy: Right. Although it's nice if you can take home the pot.

Scott: It is nice, yes. So, last question I have for you. I know you and your wife are pretty much best friends. You guys are open and honest with each other and have a great relationship. Much like my wife, where I talk to her and we discuss things I wouldn't with anyone else. How important is it, though, to have somebody other than your wife, another guy, as a close friend to be able to talk things through? Whether it's things relationally, whether it's things you're struggling with as a man in your faith or as a father. Obviously, our wives are our best friends, we married them, but how important is that other piece for you?

Randy: I look at my wife as an extension of myself, meaning anything that goes on in my head, I should be able to talk about with her, without the fear of retribution, without the fear of rejection and that sort of thing. I think it's very important to have that other person that speaks in your life because my wife and I see eye to eye on a lot of things, and we made a commitment and a vow to approach things in our life from the position of what's best for us rather than what's best for me. So in dealing with another or thinking about the importance of somebody on the outside to speak individually to me or for Robyn to speak individually to her, those people need to be there because they can bring a different viewpoint, one that is not jilted by my and my partner's time together. Where Robyn and I think a lot alike in a lot of things, I need somebody that doesn't always think like me to give me a varied viewpoint.

71

Scott: Somebody who is outside the forest and can see the trees.

Randy: Right, and in dealing with husbands and wives, sometimes if there is frustration or friction in a marriage, I think it's very important to get an outsider's viewpoint about the things that are going on, where you're maybe bumping heads with your wife on something, to get somebody else's viewpoint to say I don't care if I'm wrong or if she's wrong. In the end, hopefully I'm wrong, because I can change me. You can't always change somebody else, but I can always change me, so if the problem is with me, by all means, and that's where I want it to be, I need to know about it.

Scott: Yep, so you can actually do something about it and start making that attempt at imperfect progress. Is there anything else that you can think of that you think would be beneficial to guys when it comes to friendships?

Randy: Be honest. Don't blow smoke up somebody's ass. If somebody asks for your opinion, give them your opinion, because they've asked for it. Your opinion is not there to support what they believe. Your opinion is there to balance what they believe. Which, I mean, it could be okay, and you could have a supporting opinion, but you could also have an opinion that says, "Hey, did you think about this?" "Oh, no, I didn't think about that." So a friend is not going to always support everything that his friend brings to him. I don't think there's anybody who thinks that much alike or can think things through. Who was it in the book, How to Win Friends and Influence People? Was it one of the Roosevelts, Teddy Roosevelt, or something who says, "I think I'm right like 50 percent of the time." That means I'm wrong 50 percent of the time, and somebody needs to tell me that, but it's important that you have that spirit about you that can hear you might be wrong about this and you need to think about this. A lot of men can't do that. They can't fathom to think that they could be wrong about something when in fact they really can be.

Scott: They take it as an attack on them as a person instead of seeing it as something about their character that they can change.

Randy: Or just an idea. I always appreciated when we sat down at work to do the annual reviews. When I was being reviewed by my boss, I would always remind him that I'm looking for where I need to change instead of just a pat on the back for what I've done well. So, I don't want my reviews to be all roses and great. I love great reviews, but come to me with something that I need to change, and don't think that you're going to offend me by saying you might want to change this or here is the place you want to improve. It's very hard for many people to do that.

Scott: Or for people to hear it.

Randy: Well, it's hard for people to say it. It's hard for people to tell you where you need to improve.

Scott: I was talking with Kevin Wilson earlier today about fatherhood and how our reactions as dads when our boys or our kids come to us with something determines their next response or how they're going to come to us the next time. And I think it's the same way with friendships. If you come to me and say, "You know what, Scotty, here's something I'm noticing lately. Okay, is this true?" Am I seeing it or do you see it or is this something that, my reaction to you coming to me with that is going to determine whether or not it's worth it for you to do it again? And so I think as the person who is getting it and receiving it, at the very least being able to say, it's kind of like, "Thank you, sir, may I have another?" It's not necessarily that, it's thank you, and it doesn't matter if you agree with it or not at that point. At that point, you just need to accept it and then think on it.

Randy: So many times, and I've even had this conversation with Robyn about being offended, about don't be offended when somebody has the guts to come to you and say, "XYZ."

Scott: It's actually quite a dang honor!

Randy: Yes, it shows trust that you're not going to fly off the handle. It shows vulnerability, that they're willing to be vulnerable enough to say that to you and face what retribution might come back their way...like you said, their response is going to determine how involved you are willing to be in the future.

CHAPTER 5

MAN UP IN YOUR MARRIAGE

Even if you aren't married, this is going to be a chapter you need! MAN UP and pay attention! If you are married, there may be all kinds of things going through your head right now. Maybe you are in the honeymoon phase, maybe you are long past the honeymoon phase. Maybe you are in the ready-to-throw-in-the-towel phase! Believe me, I've been there. This chapter isn't about marriage counseling, but it *is* about what you have control over—you. You can make different choices than you have in the past. You have the power to change, so be willing to MAN UP in your marriage and then sit back and see what happens.

Husband of the Year

"Hey Ted, a bunch of the guys are getting together tonight for poker, are you in?"

"Nah, sorry Steve, I can't tonight. I have to go see a play with the wife. But, you know what they say…happy wife, happy life."

I don't know of many men who haven't had this type of exchange with a buddy. I don't care how good of a husband you are, no one is perfect. The question is, how often does a phase like this happen for you? Marriage is tough, and I don't know many men who haven't felt like they just got their teeth kicked in at some point in their marriage. The worst part is the number of couples out there who straight-up lie about how great their marriage is! Most times it's the same ones who gossip about other couples who are actually dishonest about having troubles when in reality, they are a hairs breath away, from complete disaster, themselves.

Why is marriage so tough at times? Well, you have two different people trying to figure out their individual identity and at the same time their identity together as a couple. Depending on how long they were single, this can be really difficult for someone who has become accustomed to not answering to anyone but themselves. Of course, marriage seems easier at first, because it's fresh, new, and exciting. But, as time wears on, the freshness and newness can get a little old and feelings become stale. Consequently, that exciting physical part can begin to wear thin as well.

If that happens, you now hope, somehow there is something emotionally and or psychologically left that the two of you can latch onto to keep things going. This may sound harsh, but it's the truth. It is the reason for cultivating more than just a physical relationship with your wife. Obviously, the physical part is important, and there are ways to keep that "fresh" and exciting, and you should work on that together. But, it can't be everything or the relationship is doomed.

Okay, let's go back to the opening lines of this chapter. Do you remember when you first started dating your wife? I will bet a lot of money the phrase "I have to..." never left your mouth. I would hope for most of us, we were so happy we found a woman who actually wanted to do something with us we wouldn't have even considered that phrase. The "happy wife, happy life" part? Nine times out of ten, that phrase is typically uttered when we are complaining about having to do something we don't want to, as we alluded to earlier.

Marriage is not always a Cialis commercial, sitting in outside bathtubs, holding hands during a sunset. Work is a big part of any marriage, and not just from one side. Are there things women can or should do better to help the marriage? Of course. They are human and make mistakes just like us. But, if you have been married any length of time, hopefully you understand that there is nothing we can do to force or change them in anyway. As I said in the beginning, we need to look at the one thing we as men can control in a marriage—ourselves! We are the only ones who have control over our words, responses, anger, criticism, complaining, forgiveness, unrealistic expectations, and everything else that originates with us.

Pay Attention

We've established, and I think everyone understands, that controlling our actions and responses is important. Just as important, if not more so, is paying attention to our wives' responses, actions, and moods. Imagine yourself driving on the freeway at seventy-plus miles per hour when you begin to hear an odd noise from your vehicle, or a funny shake or shimmy. What are the chances of that not causing concern? Do you exit as soon as possible and look for an open shop to take a peek at it? Or, if you have the skills yourself, do you begin the troubleshooting process? Of course you do—it wouldn't be smart to continue ignoring a potential for disaster. As husbands, why is it we sometimes pay more attention to the noises coming from our boats, trucks, motorcycles, or lawn mowers than we do to someone we promised to love until death do us part?

Let's look at it in a little different way. In almost every business, part of the picture is attracting new customers. The other part of the picture is retention of existing customers. If you focus on the attraction of new customers and forget about the retention piece, you are doing twice the work. You must attract twice the number of new customers to replace income due to the loss of existing customers.

In reality, this concept has some parallel to marriage. Some men think that once they get married, they don't have to put in effort anymore. It's like they went on the hunt, captured their prey, mounted it on the wall, and now they are sitting by the fireplace with their feet up thinking the work is over. Nothing could be further from the truth! Just as in business, in marriage you have to work at keeping a customer as hard as you do making a customer. If you are not paying attention and meeting the needs of your wife (your existing customer), there's a good chance she will begin to look elsewhere to have those needs met.

Not to completely change up the metaphors, but the reality is that your wife is not your trophy, she's your business partner. You wouldn't make decisions without consulting your business partner, would you? You wouldn't shun your business partner's ideas or belittle them. No, they have an equal investment, risk, and say in the business, or in this case, the relationship. If you aren't including your wife and making the effort to meet her needs, that could drive her to look elsewhere to get those needs met, and at the very least, you would a very bitter wife on your hands. And if happy wife = happy life, then bitter wife = living hell.

If you are not paying attention to what is happening in your wife's day-to-day activities, interactions with you, the kids, and her emotions, you run the high risk of missing what she needs and leaving her needs unmet. Unmet needs foster bitterness. Plus, if she is bitter, I guarantee you are not happy. And if you are bitter and unhappy, it will transfer to her.

Let's say you are already there. You haven't been paying attention and now bitterness has crept in to your relationship. How can you change that? How can you begin to know what your wife's needs are? This is where the manning up part comes in. First of all, you need to apologize. I know, I wasn't there. I don't really know whose fault it was, but trust me on this one. It doesn't really matter and it's an excellent first step! A simple, "Honey, I realize I haven't been paying attention to your emotional needs like I should and I'm sorry. I want to do better." Once you pick her jaw up off the floor, give her a kiss and continue with, "What can I do to better meet your needs and let you know that I see you as valuable to me and an equal partner in our marriage and in our home?"

Now, don't go rolling your eyes or give me any BS about, "I'm a man. I don't talk about feelings." Well, I'm a man too and I do. In fact, lots of men do. It's time we MAN UP and break the stigma that there is something wrong with men who feel and talk about their feelings. When Brenda and I were first dating, I was the one who wanted to talk about feelings way more than she did. In fact, she didn't want to talk about her feelings at all. Most of our fights would stem from this difference. I've always known that great marriages are a byproduct of great communication. That doesn't just mean talking about the kids' sports schedules or setting a budget. That means talking about how you feel and how she feels and how you can help each other feel valued and respected.

Once you've asked her about her feelings and her needs, pay attention and *listen*! Next, take action! Show her you love her, and if you don't feel it at the moment, remember that once you take action, your feelings will eventually follow.

Take Action

So what do our actions look like when we are in love? Do you remember the early days with your spouse? Did you gaze into your lover's eyes for hours and it only felt like minutes? How about feeling so secure that you didn't need constant contact yet, you would often find yourself thinking and smiling about her at random times of the day. What about driving and holding hands without saying a thing, yet you felt that deep connection through the silence. Did you guys know exactly what the other was thinking based on a certain smile, wink, nudge, or touch? Did you simply see a picture or hear her name and get that crazy feeling? Do you have times when you get mad and scream at each other, because you are passionate about them and the relationship, and that is something worth fighting for?

My goal in writing this book was not to give you a candy-coated version of a world that doesn't exist. Here is the deal though. Even though much of the previous paragraph can sound like a fairy tale type of love, it is possible. The possibility will only reveal itself through hard work and self-sacrifice. I want to be honest and talk candidly about real problems real men have and some potential real-world solutions. So let's look at some action we can take, to fan the flame of love in your marriage.

Go Old-Fashioned on Her

As years progress, some ideas and actions are either replaced because we improve on them, or they are plain forgotten. I don't know why but the action of treating a woman like a lady seems to have become a lost art. I get it, women want to be seen as equals. I have even been chastised for opening a door or saying, "Ladies first." However, I will tell you right now, my wife has never chastised me for treating her like a lady.

One of my favorite authors I have had the pleasure to meet and become friends with, Andy Andrews, talks a lot in his books about perspective. Opening doors, pulling out a chair for a woman to be seated first, helping with a coat, to name a few, is not me thinking she is weak or needs to be taken care of. These kinds of gestures are subtle ways I honor and serve her. Other ways you can treat your wife like the lady she is would be opening the car for her, or when you are going somewhere drop her off at the entrance and then go park the car. Pull out the chair for her and seat her first at a restaurant. Don't let the waiter or anyone else treat your wife better than you do!

Voice Your Love

This should have been number one, and really shouldn't have to be included in a list of things you should be doing to MAN UP for your wife. But, I've learned over the years not to assume things. Like some Christians who go to church only on Easter and Christmas, voicing your love for her shouldn't only happen on your anniversary and Valentine's Day. Holidays are for amateurs. It's obvious that as a society we are conditioned to say those three little words without thinking and without much meaning. When you say these words at a time that is least expected, it will actually hold more meaning for your wife. Like in the middle of a conversation, stop and look her in the eye and say, "I love you." Or something as simple as a walk-by "love you" (which I like to couple with a love tap to the backside) or a random text in the middle of the day can mean so much more to your wife than something that has become expected or routine. When was the last time you left a love note somewhere only your wife would find? It takes less than a minute but the impact can be quite lasting!

On a similar note, expressing love through physical touch should be done when it's least expected—like at times other than when you are in bed. Nonsexual touch is an excellent way to say "I love you" without saying a thing! A long hug, a quick squeeze, holding her hand, or a love tap randomly during the day can convey so much to your unsuspecting wife! MAN UP tip of the day...a back rub without any expectations will simply rock her world. Drop the mic.

Tell Her How Hot She Is

Think back to the first time you laid eyes on your wife and the feeling you got down south. Of course, I am talking about the butterflies in your stomach. The feeling that happens a little further south is an important part of married life too. When she dresses to impress, pay attention! Acknowledge verbally how good she looks. As husbands, we all know the land mines lurking around this topic. We've all cringed at the question, "Do you notice something different about me?" Or, "Does this dress make me look fat?" Dude, you can dig yourself a hole way deep in this scenario but I'm going to tell you right now, be careful not to even pick up the shovel! You will find you can't put it down and you'll only dig the hole deeper. Words are important, and you need to choose them wisely. Even if the outfit she is wearing is not very flattering, you never answer with a yes. A better reply might be, "Sweetheart, you could make a paper bag look amazing but the most important thing is that you are comfortable and feel your best. Is there something else you think you'd like better?" (We all know there is never just one outfit waiting to be tried on.) You could also say, "How could I possibly notice your outfit when I'm so completely lost in your eyes?" (Make sure you are gazing at her eyes.) Or, "If you want my opinion, I'd like to see what else you have in mind so I can see all the options."

Whatever you say, just make sure you are talking about the outfit, not your wife's body. You have to separate the "who" from the "what." Sort of like when you discipline kids, you communicate that the behavior was bad, not that the child was bad. You have to be clear so you don't hurt her feelings. In this case, if the outfit your wife is asking about doesn't flatter her, instead of saying, "It makes your butt look big," reply with, "I think that style or cut is probably for a different body type. You have so many other things that suit you better and do you justice!" If the outfit is the right one, respond with something like, "*You* make that outfit look good!" Whatever your response is, learn to choose your words wisely and show genuine interest. She's asking for your input for a reason. She wants you to be pleased with her appearance first and foremost. Sometimes she may not even want you to say anything. The best way to gauge if she wants your input or not is to simply ask the question, "How does that outfit make you feel?" Sometimes questions like this can help her work through her own decision without putting you in harm's way.

Seriously...Take Her Seriously

If you haven't seen the video called "It's Not About the Nail" on YouTube, take a minute now, or soon, and watch it. Many men, by nature, are fixers. We see a problem and go straight into how-do-I-solve-this mode. For whatever reason, if we don't go into this mode, we have an alternate mode called the nod and fade. We nod like we are listening, while we fade away into a completely distant galaxy. The problem with always being the problem solver is that many times our wives don't want us to solve the problem for them. Well, at least not the way we think they do. They want to talk it out. They want us to listen and show support while they sort through it. They need to know we have confidence in them to figure it out. And, if we don't intervene, they will figure it out as they talk it out. With the nod-and-fade, set aside the fact that you are just tuning her out. This one gets us into trouble, when they are actually looking for our input. Usually it sounds like this...

"Blah blah blah blah, so what do you think, honey?"

"Uh, yeah, what did you say?"

"Seriously? You weren't even listening to me were you!"

Either way, the problem has two possible layers. First, we aren't taking them seriously, and/or we aren't asking questions or communicating effectively. Again, an easy solution is to simply ask a question: "Honey, is this something you are looking for my input on or would you just like to vent?" This simple question shows you are serious about what she has to say and concerned about what she wants. The question to ask yourself is just as simple. Are you hearing or actively listening? What's the difference? Hearing is simply the act of perceiving sound by the ear. If you are not hearing-impaired, hearing simply happens. Listening, however, is something you consciously choose to do. Listening requires concentration so that your brain processes meaning from words and sentences. To help me with this process I try to remember this one thing. My wife married me as her husband, to listen and have her back. She didn't marry me as her father, to be the one telling her what to do.

Pitch the Porn

For some guys reading this, it's about to get very real. The men that do this are typically from one of two camps: either they don't care what anyone else thinks, or they'd be mortified if anyone knew they indulged in it. Porn.

So what's the problem with a little porn, right? Take some time to read the vast amount of studies out there on the problems with porn and you'll soon find out. Let's talk a little bit about why it's so addictive. Interestingly enough it starts up top, not down below. When someone watches porn, the brain releases a chemical called dopamine. Dopamine gives us a feeling of euphoria, like a high, when released. It is what's known as a neurotransmitter, which is like a highway in your brain. These neurotransmitters give signals to different areas of the brain. These signals then train the brain about what is good, bad, healthy, dangerous, helpful, and harmful. When dopamine is released in the brain, without realizing it, we are training ourselves to want a repeat of whatever it was that produced the dopamine rush.

To put it into context, orgasms trigger a dopamine rush. Whatever you are thinking about or gazing at when you orgasm is what your brain will look for to get the next hit. Makes sense now why your brain craves a repeat, right? The problem is, when someone constantly looks at porn and the brain is flooded with dopamine all the time, the brain starts to decrease dopamine receptors (little neurological sensors). (Kind of like tuning out a nag.) With the decrease in receptors the brain can't feel the rush as much anymore, and the porn that used to excite isn't so intense anymore. To get that intense feeling back there are two options: more porn or more intense porn. (This is the simplified version; it gets much more in depth.) This vicious cycle alone is cause for concern. The addictive nature is one thing, but watching this stuff on a regular basis begins to skew a person's ideas about what is normal.

And MAN UP—there is nothing normal about porn. The degradation of women, physical violence, ideals of body size/shape, and what women want undergo a slow shift from what is morally right to deplorable. And none of it is real. It's acting for the camera! Dr. Jeffrey Satinover of Princeton University, while describing porn's effect to a US Senate committee, said, "It is as though we have devised a form of heroin...usable in the privacy of one's own home and injected directly to the brain through the eyes." Think about that statement for a while. Would you be okay with your son injecting heroin as long as it was in the privacy of their own room? Would you inject heroin in the privacy of your own home? Our wives deserve more than being viewed as an object of pleasure to be used. Our daughters deserve more than to be the object of desire for men to get their fix. The argument usually heard is, "That won't happen to me, I've got it under control." I'd bet donuts to dollars the pilot of the *Hindenburg* said, "Don't worry, I've got it all under control." Probably all the way up to the point of going down in a ball of fire. Don't start playing with the heroin. If you have, quit. If you can't quit, MAN UP and seek help.

In short, by engaging in porn you are training yourself to crave and neurologically bond with a media device and not your wife. Which is really weird when you step back and think about it. Newsflash! That media device will never love you back. It will never actually meet your needs, it will only leave you longing for more. It will never care for you when you are sick or feed you when you are hungry or support you through the challenging times of life. Porn is the thief of intimacy and a perpetrator, not only on your marriage but on your wife's heart. MAN UP, protect your marriage and pitch the porn.

Stand Up for Her

I've watched over and over, in various conversations, where a wife has been verbally attacked or insulted and the husband or boyfriend stood by doing nothing. Anyone paying attention could see her look, her plea if you will, for her husband to stand up for her. Now, there are women out there who will get mad at this. They'll say, "I can stand up for myself, I don't need you to do it for me." Fair enough. I happen to be married to a very strong woman and love that about her. But, by paying attention I can tell when she wants or doesn't want me to step in on her behalf.

Be very careful here though. This does not mean you need to grab every man that looks at or talks to your wife by the throat and threaten him to within an inch of his life. Listen to the conversation and look for cues from her before jumping in to save the day. The day may not actually need saving. Getting this wrong can be embarrassing for you, her, and everyone else around. Plus, the unneeded aggression toward others may freak her out. There is a stark difference between chivalry and being an overprotective imbecile.

Forgive and Forget

There isn't a husband or wife alive who isn't driven completely nuts by something their spouse does or doesn't do. For my wife, it's my breathing when I eat. In the spring and fall, my allergies kick my butt. We have all had a cold where we are so stuffed up, the act of drinking or swallowing food is not easy. This drives my wife nuts. Granted this really is small stuff compared to some of the things we or our spouses do that drive us mad. It can be driving, talking on the phone, leaving lights on, not putting the toilet lid back up (couldn't resist), changing the thermostat, or demanding a "chick flick" and falling asleep on you ten minutes in (thus, beginning the mental dance of trying to figure out if it's worth trying to sneak away without waking her). In the grand scheme of things, we all know most of these instances are, at best, trivial in importance. The challenge is being able to shrug them off and take them for what they're worth.

Think of your relationship as a money transaction. There are things you do, or don't do, that will cost you money, and others that will deposit more into your account (debits and credits). Our goal is to end each day with more credits than debits in our account . If you can't figure out what things cause a debit and what things result in a credit, I'm not sure you were quite ready to get married in the first place. Or, as my dad once told me, "Marriage is full of battles. You need to learn quickly which of the battles are worth fighting and which are worth compromising over. If you are fighting to win, there is always going to be a loser. Is that what you want your wife to be…collateral damage?" Never fight to win…fight for the relationship and you both win. When you are wrong, and you will be, say you're sorry. I'm not talking about the sorry that comes with all kinds of lame qualifiers and excuses either. Those are not apologies, they are excuses, and they're insulting. The proper way to apologize— and if you don't mean it don't do it—is to simply say, "I'm sorry…I was wrong….Can you forgive me? What can I do to make it right?"

Date Your Wife on a Regular Basis

This is a prime example of "do what I say, not what I do." I have a little wager with myself on how long it's going to take my wife, once she reads this, to bring this specific part up. I admit this is a struggle for both of us. But, if I am going to MAN UP I need to be diligent at making this a priority. With the demands of a successful business, three boys, volunteer work, and life in general, we know firsthand how difficult this can be at times. In reality, dating your spouse serves a few important functions:

It fuels the fire for romance. They say absence makes the heart grow fonder. It can also feed forgetfulness of what you're missing.

It draws you closer. Activities shared together result in shared feelings that strengthen your bond.

It strengthens communication. If the only communicating you are doing is about kids, work, laundry, and the car that needs fixing, the boring meter on your marriage just maxed out. All of these things bring and keep you closer together and further from possible infidelity.

On that topic, I've heard more than once recently how easy it is to cheat on your spouse these days. From apps to websites, there are things and places that encourage this behavior. I'm going to propose an idea that is a completely different line of thought: it's actually harder to cheat on your spouse than it is to remain faithful. I was watching an outdoor show with my son the other night and a natural resources officer (think officer of the woods) was talking to one of the people he had stopped. He told him, "It's easier if you just tell me the truth. Do that, and you don't have to work so hard to remember exactly how the other lies you have told me went." If you apply this to your marriage, the same thing is true. If you took half the energy it would require to cover up cheating and put it into the things we are talking about here, you wouldn't have any desire to step out on your spouse in the first place.

One last tip on dating your wife. Don't leave the planning entirely up to her. MAN UP and take some initiative yourself. You would be amazed at the results that simple step can yield.

Are You Interested in Her Interests?

No, you don't need to develop a love for shoes and purses. There are very few "unicorn couples"—those perfect couples who love all the same things and do *everything* together. In fact, I don't think that is altogether even healthy. We are all different, and no one should be forced to give up an interest (as long as it's healthy) because somebody else doesn't share the same feelings about it. What I am saying is if you have zero common interests, that is a red flag.

When my wife and I went through our rough spell, a piece of advice given to us was to expand our common interests. We had gotten into the marriage rut of work, kids, and duties. There was a serious lack of doing things just for fun. On a whim I suggested she come snowmobiling with some friends of ours. I honestly thought, "Hey, at least I came up with an idea, even though I doubt she'll like it." She turned into an animal on the trails and we had an absolute blast together.

I grew up on a farm, am an avid outdoorsman, love shooting sports, and would rather be outside than in. Brenda grew up in suburbia—nothing against it, just starkly different worlds. I have offered to include her in all of my outdoor exploits but never pushed it on her. This past year we went to Front Sight, a firearms training facility we are lifetime members of. Brenda was very apprehensive about going, but by the time the course was finished, her confidence had grown so much we had a new common interest. I applaud her for trying something new and getting outside of her comfort zone.

As men we need to get outside of our comfort zone and try new things that are important to our wives as well. Brenda loves to scuba dive and is open water certified. I on the other hand would rather brush the teeth of a mountain lion that hasn't eaten in a week. To say I have a fear of the water would be akin to someone saying they are kind of pregnant. Okay, well there is the general fear of the water and then there is the fear of stuff in the water that will eat you.

Fast-forward to being in Mexico and Brenda seeing a dive "shack." She says, "Let's try it, you'll never know unless you try." I say okay, but I faintly remembered something about not being able to dive like everyone else if you have asthma. As we are talking to the guys in the shack, I make sure to be very clear about my asthma…insert cough here. Their response? "No worries, man…that's not true." Pretty sure to this day they lied right to my face. We proceeded to go straight to forty feet after a five-minute lesson at twelve feet. People have asked me what was it like. Well, combine the fear of not being able to breathe, claustrophobia, and creatures of the deep that eat you and I explain it like this: it was sheer terror, interrupted by moments of bliss. All of my oxygen was used up in the first half hour, and everyone else continued to dive for at least another forty-five minutes while I got acquainted with a couple cervezas back on the boat.

I have lost track of the number of miles I have logged, in tow, while Brenda shopped on the various exotic islands we have visited. Even though our first outing on bicycles together as a couple resulted in an extensive ER visit, we have bought bicycles as a family for getting out and staying active together. You may want to take dancing lessons together, buy or rent motorcycles, try cooking classes, or go on a hunting trip. Once again, MAN UP and take the initiative to ask her what it is she would like to do. This is where the rubber meets the road though. She may suggest something that pushes you way outside your boundary of comfort, like diving…in the ocean…or shopping. Go into it with an open mind and focus on the time you are spending with her. No complaining, whining, or grumbling, no matter how much you think you aren't going to like it. You may even end up with a new hobby or passion you never would have seen yourself being interested in.

Watch Your Punctuation!

No, I'm not going to teach you how to write a love letter to your wife, but I am going to lay out a few sentences I want you to read. Think about what they really mean, based on the punctuation…

"I'm sorry honey, but I got busy and forgot."

"I love you, but right now you are really irritating me."

"I agree with you, but I think you need to do this instead."

What do you see with these sentences? I'm sure you see there is a "but" in every one of them. The "but" and comma, to put it as simply as I can, are nothing but excuses. They completely contradict how we started the sentence. Seriously? "I love you, but…." All that says is, I love you but not really, and here is why. "I'm sorry, but...." I'm sorry, but let me try to make it hurt less that I couldn't remember something important to you. "I agree, but...." I agree with you, but I'm just kidding and here's why. Words do matter, and I guarantee your wife will notice if you start watching what and how you say things. How different do you think she would respond, if instead you said it like this:

"I'm sorry, honey, I forgot, my bad. How can I make it up to you?"

"I understand what you are saying. I don't necessarily agree with it, and I'd like to talk about it more."

This one is the big one: the only punctuation that should come after "I love you" is either a period or exclamation point. "I love you. Because of that, I need to step back for a second and calm down, so I don't say something stupid."

Recently I had the pleasure of sitting down with a guy I respect and who I feel is crushing the area of being a good husband. Verick has been married to his wife Crystal for nineteen years. They have four children together ranging in age from six to sixteen and he has some great insights to share.

MAN UP in Your Marriage: Interview with Verick Burchfield

Scott: How did you and Crystal meet?

Verick: Man, it was like the most ultimate setup ever. Actually, we met at a gas station. A buddy of mine and I were supposed to go to a Disciple Now weekend to be teachers with his college group, and so I was supposed to work that weekend. Crystal actually was supposed to work that weekend as well. She was in that college group, and they were meeting us halfway in Tuscaloosa at a gas station. We pulled up, and she walked over to us because she knew my friend Brandon. But she didn't walk up to Brandon, she walked right over to me, and she goes, "You've got the most beautiful eyes I've ever seen." Like, never met this girl, but she was gorgeous, right? So I was telling the guys this weekend, I've been married to Crystal nineteen years, but we've known each other for almost twenty-one. I still remember that moment, the teal shirt and the overalls, short bobbed hair, and the boots that she was wearing, and I knew that weekend she was going to be my wife. So that was a pretty poignant moment. We talked pretty much that whole weekend. I even told my friend that weekend, "That's my wife, I'm going to marry her." So basically, any free time I had, I rattled off twenty questions to her, kind of like going down my list of what I was looking for in a wife. It was like she was in the inquisition, right? But she liked me, and so thankfully she was gracious enough to get through that. I knew she was the one and then it took me a while to convince her of that and I had to counsel her away from a couple of suitors who were blinded by her beauty as well.

Scott: Let's dive right in to the meat of why we are here. With the title of the book, MAN UP, what would you say are the top two things that are necessary to MAN UP as a husband?

Verick: These are things I am working on all the time, so they are pretty much on the top of my head: leadership, accountability, and humility. I would say those are the top three. Leading, not expecting your wife to lead all the time even though she can be an amazing leader. Being humble enough when she sees things in you that need work, to move forward in those things, instead of getting upset and getting frustrated. This is a willingness to continually work on yourself, asking and allowing her to hold you accountable in the marriage relationship since you are one. When she holds you accountable, you're holding yourself accountable if you're humble enough to do that, and so those are the top three things I think that are the most important.

Scott: I am going to delve in a little bit more to accountability then since you brought that up, and I like that word. Obviously, there are things that we are going to be accountable to our spouse on and about. There are certain things we would feel comfortable telling our spouse but nobody else in the world, they know us better than anyone else. But, how important is an accountability piece with other men who you trust and are close to you, for your marriage?

Verick: I think that's huge, and actually, I have three guys that I talk to on a regular basis about that. We check on each other almost every single day, just hey, how's it going? Praying for your family. Is there anything that we can pray about for you guys? I haven't talked to you in a while. Is everything okay? It's vitally important that you have other men holding you accountable to be active in your marriage, be a leader in your marriage, and to be there. These are the guys, if your wife needs to call you out and you're not listening, she can reach out to and say, hey, can you help get him in line? I have had that in place for a while. The piece of lifting each other up and being there to walk alongside you during the hard times is vitally important. Men sharpen each other, and while my wife and I talk about everything, having other men challenge you and really push you in areas that you may not want to be pushed is extremely important.

Scott: So you mentioned that these are things you struggle with every single day. I think it's important for guys to understand as they're reading how many times either of us have perfected leadership, accountability, and humility in our relationship with our wives.

Verick: I could bring her in here, and I think she'd have a hard time saying I have ever perfected any of it at any time. It's difficult, it really is, because we get in a rut. There are certain things, whether it's not holding your kids accountable to something, not leading, not daily doing devotions, not taking that time to pour into them from the word of God, and that's something that we dealt with. Guys will do really well for two or three weeks, and then we will disappear for a week, and so it gives not only our kids a mixed message, but it gives our wives a mixed message as well as. Are we really going to be a leader? And usually, after about a week of that, she comes to you and goes, "Hey, I need you to step up," which we often let offend us. This leads to us needing to apologize and we end up starting this whole cycle over. Obviously, our goal should be to break that cycle, and just like you say in your book, man up and actually just walk these things out on a daily basis no matter how hard they are, no matter how frustrating they are. We need to get things done because ultimately our job is not to please our wife, but our job is to please God. The cool thing is, the effect of pleasing God is going to be a wife that is pleased and harmony in your home.

Scott: Just from watching your interaction with your wife and knowing you as a man, I know how much you care for and love your wife. For men out there who are either newly married or thinking about getting married, what are ways we as men can show our wives we love them? In the Bible, it says to treat your wife as Christ would the church, but what does that look like in real life for what we would do?

Verick: I think it actually obviously has to start right there. When you look through that verse and it says to treat your wife like Christ treated the church in that he laid down his life for her, right? So that is where we start and I think most guys would say, I am willing to lay down my life for my wife. You would jump in front of a car for your wife, you would take a bullet for your wife, but I think the true aspect of laying down your life for your wife is the willingness to bypass your own agenda for your wife.

I'm going to bring Young Living into this for just a little bit. When Crystal's business took off in Young Living, I was still working full-time in the emergency room, fifty hours a week. As her business started growing and growing and growing, there came a time where her agenda was becoming more important than mine, and I had to be willing to lay that down so that she could step up and shine and have that time in the spotlight.

Many times it ends up being cyclical. She had stayed at home for the last fifteen years taking care of the kids and the house, while I was working full-time. I had to be willing to be humble and step out of the limelight, if you will, of running an emergency room and everything that comes with that, and watch her elevate and move into what God had called her to. I think especially for newlyweds, my advice is to always be willing to communicate and work with your wife's agenda. I'm not saying that she is going to lord that over you or she is going to be in charge or anything like that, but seeing who she is and being willing to lay down your life for her even in some of the minor details. You accomplish this by doing things for her, writing notes for her, surprising her by taking her on a trip, or to dinner, and doing those things on a regular basis so that she knows that she's loved.

Back before I got married, a pastor friend of mine gave me some really great advice in marriage. He said, "Chase her smile." Three words. He said, "That's all the marriage advice I need to give you." I said oh, that's really not a whole lot. He said if you think about it, it's everything. I have been trying to do that in our marriage ever since the beginning. Now have I failed at times, miserably at points? Yeah, yeah, I really have, and it seemed like I was chasing her tears more than chasing her smile at times. But, through it all, I think if you are willing to, and are always looking to put your wife's interests first, it is not only going to help her to feel valued, which is so important, but it is also going to bleed over into other areas. Your children are going to see your wife as valued, they are going to see how to lead, and they are going to see how to treat their wives.

I once saw Jimmy Evans, who is a famous marriage expert, and he was telling a story about this guy who lived in an old farming community. The time period was like hundreds of years ago, and it was a time where a guy, when he wanted to marry a woman, would take two cows and go to see her dad.

They would then make a trade, like for that of a dowry. The girl he is interested in is shunned and one of the ugliest girls in town. He walks up to her dad and offers him seven cows for his ugly daughter. Her dad looks at him and says, "Why would you offer seven cows for my daughter? I know she's not that pretty." He replied, "I'm just offering you seven cows."

Years later, the father went to visit, and the door was answered by an absolutely gorgeous, beautiful lady. He had never seen a woman so pretty. What he eventually found out was he did not recognize his own daughter. He said to the husband, "We never thought she would look this pretty. Did you see something in her or what did you do to make her look like that?" He said, "It wasn't only what I saw in her. Most guys would have spent one to two cows, but I wanted her to know what it meant to be a seven-cow wife. I wanted her to know that she was the most important and that she was worth more than any other woman in this village." It was that important to him, and this illustration showed her that she was the most important thing and so valued that it actually changed who she was.

If I've got any advice for the reader...do that. If you're going to be excessive in anything in your marriage, it's doing things for your wife. I'm not saying go broke over it. I'm just saying get out of the box. Think bigger than you really are. I remember when Crystal was sick, there is only so much you can do to help. We were trapped in our house. We couldn't travel a whole lot, and we were having money problems, but I could write. Right before we went on a trip to Boston, I started writing her a book for Christmas. I figured, if I can't afford to buy her anything for Christmas, at least I can write her a book. It was fun writing it, but what she saw was three or four months' worth of hard work being put into a Christmas gift. It really didn't cost me anything other than time, but it meant a lot to her. Investing that time into your wife really is the most important thing, and to me, what's what laying your life down for your wife means.

Scott: So date nights. Yay or nay?

Verick: We try to do them as much as we can. It's a little different for us. We are in Kansas City. We don't have family out here, and we live in the middle of nowhere, so it's difficult for us to get a babysitter that wants to drive thirty-five miles each way and watch the kids. So our kids actually now are starting to get a little bit older where we've got older teenagers that are able to help, but usually date night for us is just time away where we can talk. We connect, and we would step away from business as much as possible. We can talk about the kids, we can talk about our future and our plans, but I wish we had more of them. That's a scenario, actually, that I need to work on.

As I said, as the kids are getting older, we're able to do more. We're focusing in more on Crystal's health right now so we are not doing too much, but I could do better on doing them in the house even, but yeah, date nights are a must. Some people schedule them. Crystal is not one that wants to schedule a date night because she does not want it to ever become routine, so I understand that as well. She said because she might be sick so she doesn't want to, with her health the way it is right now, you don't want to schedule something and then…so we have to kind of go on the fly. But as far as date nights go, they are very important because it's stopping to reconnect. A lot of people work outside of the home and they're going separate ways, and they're busy. Crystal and I are here, and so we are able to communicate a lot, whether it's just being down in our basement and me working out and she's taking a sauna and we just decide to talk and work things out, that's one thing, but yeah, it's vitally important.

Scott: So for the guys out there, how important is it that they take an active role and actually plan one of these dates themselves?

Verick: Actually, I'm a little guilty in that area. Truthfully, I've been a little bit in a rut with school and with work and getting laser focused on doing those things, I have let that slide a little bit. I can tell you what though. When I do it, it makes a huge difference. I think the last one that I planned was a few months ago, like a big planned one, and so that says a lot about me, that I need to step that part back up again.

Scott: It's been a few months since you have done one. I'm sure there are a lot of guys reading this, and it's been years or they have never done it. I think it's a challenge. This relates well to the subject of men owning their own health. We will take control and ownership of our trucks and our crap and toys, but yet taking ownership of scheduling something for the one who captured our hearts is like…"Oh boy, what do I do?" None of us are alone in this; it is an area that I should be making imperfect progress in, not zero progress.

I want you to think of all the guys you know, your buddies like Les and Andy and when you talk, what is the most common source of tension for a marriage, that comes up?

Verick: I think in the microcosm that we're in and the business that we're in, it's two things. I think with the couples who are just starting out, the biggest tension is money and then wanting to see results, and/or not seeing results in their time frame. As their wife becomes more successful, and as any wife becomes more successful, I think the biggest bone of contention is each other's role. Whose role is what? Is the guy still the provider? What happens if roles change? And so I think those are the two biggest things, money and identifying the role of each person in the marriage. If those aren't identified, and the money isn't talked about or taken care of, it adds so much stress and tension. Children in the mix are always going to add stress, and I think that is a given. Knowing your role and being okay with that is very important. If your role is to be a helper in a business or the helper in whatever with your marriage, it doesn't mean that you're weaker, it doesn't mean that you're lacking. I think guys really have to figure out what their identity is, and finding our identity in Christ is one of the biggest things that has helped me, because I know that I am a son of God and have been cared for so much and that God sent His Son to die for me. The other roles that we have to take on, whether we like them or not, should not shake us to our core and destroy our marriages if we are secure in our identity. Even if it is stepping down from a level that we deem important to a level we don't feel is as important.

Scott: I think you've touched on some really big...that level that we think is important.

Verick: If you're taking care of things...like when I left my job and I came home—taking care of what meant the most to Crystal, and what ministered to her the most was if I had the dishes and the laundry done, the kids taken care of, and the school work done. She didn't care if I was bringing money in. She didn't care if I was willing to teach to our team. She wanted to know that those other things were taken care of, because that gave her security. To provide security in no matter what situation is going on is one of the biggest roles of a husband.

Scott: I think you just touched on something really important. I think it boils down to communicating what that security piece is. Like for Crystal, that security piece was knowing that the laundry was done, the house was clean, the kids were taken care of, food was on the table. However not all women's security piece is the same. When I look at my experience of leaving my job and joining my wife, the security piece for her was, how am I adding to the financial capability of the family? She could have cared less about the laundry, it could have piled up for weeks or months, probably years. She would have just bought and brought new underwear and socks home. To succeed in a transition like this, we need to have those open, honest communication episodes about the money, roles, expectations, and about what each person really wants, instead of thinking, "Well, I'm pretty sure that all women want this so that's what I'm gonna do."

Verick: Yeah, you don't ever want to assume what your wife wants. The most honest time that you may get is if she's mad at you. If she is saying I need you to do this, I need you to do that, or I need you to step it up in a certain area, she's not making those things up. It may be that you are just hearing them for the first time because the volume got loud enough so listen. Even during an argument, listen, because that's probably when you're going to hear what you need to work on the most!

Scott: Great segue since the next question I had was, how do you listen to her?

Verick: I try to listen before we get to the argument stage, but in every marriage, you argue. Seriously, Crystal and I talk all the time. Literally at night, we basically have to tell each other to shut up and go to bed because we'll just talk and talk and talk, and God's really blessed us with a marriage we feel comfortable to do that in. I enjoy spending time with her and hearing what she has to say, and I'm interested in what she has to say, and so one thing that we as husbands have to do is make sure that our wife's voice is the loudest and most important one that's speaking into us. We can have accountability to friends and other people, but we don't live with any of them. We must listen to her and be willing to listen, even if she doesn't even want you to talk. She may talk for two hours and not want you to say a thing. You need to understand that and don't try to fix it. You just listen to her, but listen, not listening for when she's done so you can do…but listening for what is in her heart, because she can tell instantly if you're listening for another reason.

Scott: And they do test us too, don't they? Here's a little tip for you guys out there. If you're sitting there thinking that hey, I can just zone out and I don't have to worry about it, there's a test after their presentation, and they're going to find out whether or not you were listening.

So kind of along the same lines of what we were talking about as far as listening, that role piece, the money piece, security piece, being her support, being your wife's support versus being her father. Speak a little bit about that, if you will.

Verick: That is huge. I've never heard a wife tell Crystal or I've never heard Crystal tell me that she wants me to be her dad. Like I want you to set all the rules, I want you to do all this. That's not our role. We are, when we get married, we become one, and that authority, while it is shared and while we may have the ultimate voice or the ultimate vote in our marriage if that's the way that you guys walk things out, it's the way we walk things out, I never lord that over her. The last thing that Crystal wanted to do was marry her dad. The last thing any woman wants to do is marry their dad. I believe since God made my wife for me, he also made my wife to be the completion of the things that are going to make me a better person, and so if I don't listen to her and if I'm not supporting her, I'm really cutting out part of my growth and my maturity because if I'm lording over her and I'm just dictating to her and giving her things that she has to do, it's not going to help me to be a better man and to be a better father and better leader. Trying to be the ruler of the house/relationship is going to damage our relationship. She's not going to want to open up to me if I'm the only one who gets input, but she is going to be willing to work with me if I'm willing to support and work with her. It's just like in any business or with a team. If you're the only one giving the rules, then that may work for three months, and then you're going to be alone, and nobody is going to talk to you. It works the exact same way in a marriage. That's why I like the book by Patrick Lencioni, The Five Dysfunctions of a Team. It works well for your business, but it also works really well for your family. You've gotta have those foundations. You've gotta work within those, and most of all, you have to have those in your life.

Scott: I'm going to end it with one last question. I bring this up because in my mind, for a lot of guys the struggle is real, and it's how do you keep your eyes and thoughts from wandering? I mean, let's face it. We're never going to be perfect in that realm either. It doesn't give us a get-out-of-jail-free card where it's like, okay, well you're not perfect anyway so go ahead and look or go ahead and comment or go ahead and let your thoughts go, but...One of the areas that I respect you in immensely, and honestly, I have interviewed everybody I respect for certain areas of their life. You I respect for multiple areas of your life, but this one in particular. And I think there's things that men can learn from you. You have insight and wisdom in this area when it relates to your life, and so, what do we do?

Verick: The first thing, and this is something that I have dealt with before, that I struggled with before I met Crystal, and usually if you struggle with things before you meet your wife, you bring some of those things in. I did, and we dealt with those, and we worked with those for years in our marriage. Thankfully, the Lord has worked and delivered in those areas, but I would say the way that you do that is by keeping open lines, one of the first things, keeping an open line. When a husband gets bitter, when we harbor anger, frustration, and resentment toward the one we love, our wife, then that is going to set us up for being discontented. And when it comes down to it, when we choose to do those things, when we are looking the other way or when we're doing whatever, it comes out of a heart of discontentment with the blessing that God has given us. That's where it starts.

It goes back to chasing your wife's smile. It goes back to pouring into your relationship, figuring out and settling it, that your wife is the most important thing outside of your relationship with God, and then going all in with that and just loving her, choosing to love her, and choosing to know and to settle that she is that one. When you do that, it really makes it easier because she becomes that focus, right? When you want to keep that focus proper, you're not going to put your wife as an idol. You're not going to raise her up above where God is because that's not healthy either, but I think communication and keeping your anger, being willing to work through arguments when you can the most, because usually when guys are going to do that, it's out of a reaction. They're frustrated, they're angry, there's lack of communication in a relationship. Those are the things that are usually what sets a guy up for failure. And so if you can actively work on those things, then I think you're going to have much more success.

There Is No "Take" in Love

One last thought on being the husband of the year. As Jerry Seinfeld says, "Being a good husband is like being a good stand-up comic—you need ten years before you can even call yourself a beginner." Remember, it's all about imperfect progress. There's going to be days when you're killin' it, and days when you're gettin' killed. Your goal is to make the number of days you're killin' it outnumber the days you're getting killed. Screwing up isn't a matter of if...it's when. Get over it now and be okay with trying to be the best version of a screwup you can by remembering this fact. Living out true love is not a give-and-take, and as hard as it can be, there is no "take" in love. When you love someone, and I mean really love them, your mentality is not one of, "How can you help me?" The attitude you have or should have is one of, "Lay it all on me." Whatever you are dealing with, whatever you are struggling with, lay it on me. My shoulders can handle it.

If you are reading this and you are still single, I have one piece of advice for you when it comes to the question of, "How will I ever find the right woman?" If you forget about finding the right woman and focus on being the right man, you will never need to ask that question.

CHAPTER 6

MAN UP AS A FATHER

When you become a dad, you are given a gift of power that lasts approximately sixteen years. Somewhere around that time things begin to change. Unfortunately, there is no way to accurately predict precisely when you will lose that power either. The good news is that some of the power may eventually return, but it is dependent on your child.

The power I am referring to is that of a Hero Dad. All dads have it, and this power should be wisely used. It has the ability to lift up, encourage, soothe, and heal. However, it also has the power to injure severely or even kill a spirit. Unfortunately for some, the hero in their story abandons them and/or their family, ends up abusing them, or is just checked out. This can happen in either a physical or emotional way. Honestly, I'm not sure if one is worse than the other. I am lucky and grateful my dad did none of the above.

In the midst of raising three boys, maintaining a marriage, and building businesses, I understand the things in life, as men, that pull on our time. Growing up, the idea of family vacation time for us was dad taking vacation from work and getting things done around the farm. Like other kids my age, I would have loved to have a boat and gone to the lake on the weekends. However, I believe the work ethic dad engrained into us kids at a young age, both by modeling and demanding it, had a direct impact, both good and bad, on where and who I am today. I struggle to take time from things "that need to get done," to do things my boys want to do. It is hard to change the mentality that was instilled in me that "playing happens when the work is done." But, what I have started to slowly understand is there is time for work and there is time for connection and play. By being honest about how much something really needs to be done now, a balance can be struck between work and play.

This concept was made apparent to me in the oddest of places...a chiropractic conference. The speaker was talking about how people who say they can't afford the care recommended just don't want the care. He referenced how they can find the money for vacations, TVs, cars, and so on, but not for care they need. It often wasn't that they couldn't afford care, they simply didn't place enough value on the care to warrant shelling out the money for it. This premise got me thinking about more than just the care of my patients. It got me thinking about life and questioning where I am putting my value. Was I valuing the look of a well-manicured lawn over twenty minutes of tossing the ball around with my boys? Did a clean shop matter more than a curious mind? Was I teaching them that life can be fun and enjoyed or boring and nothing but work? I am constantly trying to keep this at the front of my mind; it is the only way I can change it.

Just the other day I was walking to my shop from the house and my oldest, Wyatt, was outside, playing *Alone* or *Survivor*, with his new Christmas hatchet (survival shows are a favorite for us to watch together). He yelled, "Hey Dad, look I'm chopping down this dead tree with my new hatchet!" Without breaking stride, I casually responded with a "Good job, Wyatt" and continued toward the shop. For some reason, I stopped and looked back. As I watched him work at getting this tree down, I felt that nudge deep inside and turned. I made my way through the snow to where he was working at the edge of the woods and asked if he wanted some help. He looked up with a quizzical look he gets sometimes and said, "Am I doing this right, Dad?" After a few quick tips on what he could do better and some questions to make sure he was remembering the safety tips, he got back to chopping.

Soon you could hear the telltale cracking of the tree about to fall. With a little nudge from him, down it came. As I turned to continue my trek to the shop, the smile and look of pride on his face was worth so much more than whatever it was I so desperately needed to get done in the shop before. Later that night, all three boys and I had a little winter campfire with the wood Wyatt had chopped and gathered. We roasted s'mores and listened to him retell the story of how he chopped the wood we were using with his new hatchet. After the fire, as I was tucking him into bed, he said, "Dad, thanks for teaching me how to use my new hatchet today."

Heroes look for opportunities to be a hero, to serve someone in need. As fathers, are we looking for those opportunities to be the hero? I can guarantee you this, our kids are giving us opportunities every single day to live up to the hero they start off seeing us as. These are not requests to leap a building in a single bound or destroy an asteroid hurtling toward earth. They are simple requests like: Can you teach me how to ride a bike? Will you wrestle with me? Can you snuggle with me at bedtime? Can you help me with my homework? Can you teach me how to throw and hit a ball? The list of simple hero acts is only limited by your willingness to see them. The best part? In the eyes of our kids, answering these simple calls is right up there with leaping a building in a single bound.

Every parent remembers the day at the hospital when their first child was born. How someone was always checking in on you and your wife, simply making sure things were going okay. Usually, this happened right when you all finally fell asleep. You also remember the day they walked you both to the door with your newborn and said "good luck." If I'm honest, part of me was thinking, "Finally we can get out of here." The other part was freaking out thinking, "What? We've never done this before...where's the owner's manual?" I didn't know how to be a dad yet.

What I have had to learn and be okay with, especially raising kids, is learning from my mistakes. I remember one particular lesson I learned during the time when my wife started building her business from home and was leaving to teach classes in the evenings. We were talking with friends and I mentioned how I was learning the ropes of "babysitting." If looks could kill, I wouldn't be writing this now. Both wives proceeded to educate me, on the face that I'm not a babysitter as the parent. The whole time, my friend was sitting there with a smirk on his face and the look of, "Sorry, dude, you're on your own." Once I stopped and thought about what they were saying, it made sense. They were one hundred percent right.

Let's take a look at *Webster's* definition of babysit: "To care for children usually during a short absence of the parents." *Webster's* definition of father is: "A man who has begotten a child." *Webster's* gets the "deed" portion of it right but is so lacking in what a dad truly is. With that definition, those who do the deed and bolt are still technically fathers, but they are nothing resembling a true dad, and certainly no hero.

How can we maximize our time in the position of hero to our children? What are some steps we can take to model it effectively for our sons? In the same way, when we show our daughters what good dads are really like, we show them what to look for in a husband.

Love Trumps Everything

I chose this first because if you fail at everything else but nail this one, your kids will most likely have half a chance at turning out pretty darn good. Okay, if I were you, I'd be sitting there right now thinking, "Wow, what a revelation. Can you be any more vague?" So, let's look at some specifics that I doubt anyone would argue with…

Love is patient, love is kind. It does not envy, it does not boast, it is not proud. It does not dishonor others, it is not self-seeking, it is not easily angered, it keeps no record of wrongs. Love does not delight in evil but rejoices with the truth. It always protects, always trusts, always hopes, always perseveres. I like this definition of love found in I Corinthians 13:4–7. This is what we as dads should be striving to have our love for our kids look like and model for them as they grow. Can't really improve on those words, other than reminding us all, it's not just our kids that deserve that definition of love.

You Are Not the Babysitter

As I mentioned above, we are a parent or a dad, not a babysitter. In every house there are things that need to get done. At our house, my wife doesn't shovel snow or mow grass, and with three able-bodied boys and me around, she shouldn't have to. Unless that's what her heart desires. That's funny, the thought of Brenda begging for a chance to shovel snow—it actually made me laugh out loud. I say this to recognize there are some things that each of us will naturally gravitate toward when it comes to these household duties. But, those duties are decided together based on strengths and weaknesses you discuss as a couple. I was a master at the quick diaper change with the kids, but I'm also a sympathetic puker, so that was Brenda's job.

A great leadership principle is: never ask someone to do something you aren't willing to do yourself. Unless it's vomit, then all bets are off! If we model this for our kids with the household duties, they already have a leg up on most of the other kids in society. We are moms and dads, different, yet together we are parents. Unless things have changed since the birth of our last son, he didn't pop out with a note from God delineating which of us got certain responsibilities in caring for our children.

Lengthen Your Fuse

As I wrote that, I had a twinge of guilt. I struggle with this the most... and guess what? So did my dad, and his dad. Do you know what having a temper is? Plain and simple, it's an excuse. I struggle with this every single day I'm a dad, and I'm guessing I will continue to work on it till the day I die. The worst part about having a short fuse is when the bomb goes off and one of your kids gets hit with the shrapnel.

Don't get me wrong, there is a time for discipline and to let your kids know you're angry. But, when you can see in their eyes that you have injured them with your explosion, there is no greater hurt that I have felt. Take the time to leave the room or send your child to their room. Both of these will give you a chance to cool down. My wife and I use the code word "fuse," which I invite and encourage her to to say to me in these situations. We all need to be held accountable and I know that when she uses this word, I need to take a step back and breathe. Having a strategy like this doesn't mean you are weak. Strength is knowing when you need accountability and giving someone else the power and permission to keep you on the right path.

Apologize When You Are Wrong

About a year ago our youngest was playing with his cousin upstairs while the adults were chatting. If you have kids, you can probably guess what's coming next. My niece lets out a scream and runs downstairs crying with her finger bleeding. When we asked her what happened, she tells us our youngest hit her with a play sword. I run upstairs, grab him by the arm, and drag him to his room. I didn't even give him a chance to tell his side of the story. Remember that whole short fuse thing? I laid into him about hitting girls, being a bully, gave him the discipline I thought he deserved, and put him to bed early.

After getting back downstairs, I asked his cousin what happened. (Should have done that first, right?) She told me his sword hit her finger, which pinched it against her sword, as they were having a pretend sword fight. My heart sunk, but I knew what I had to do. I did the walk of shame, back up to my son's room, where he was still doing the ugly cry. I sat him up, gave him a hug, and told him: "Dad was wrong, I am sorry. Can you forgive me?" The part that felt like someone plunged a knife into my heart and twisted it and taught me the biggest lesson was his response. Through tears and sobs I heard, "That's okay, Dad, I still love you!"

Be a big enough man to admit when you are wrong, apologize, and model correct behavior for your kids.

Be Present

"Present" is an interesting word. Do you know the best present you could give your kids? I'll give you a clue. In the past two sentences, I've said it twice. Being fully *present* and attentive to your kids is the best *present* you could give them. I try to think of it by remembering PTC (present time consciousness), being fully in the moment with no distractions.

I remember as a kid when Dad got his first bag phone. For the younger generation reading, this was the first cell phone. It had to be plugged into the cigarette lighter, was similar to holding a shoebox, and made today's healthcare costs look like peanuts if you actually had to call someone on it. Today we all have a computer in our pockets that is faster and does more than what NASA had available during the Apollo 11 mission to the moon! It's a great thing, right?

Like most things if used properly, yes they are. Unfortunately, if you spend any time out in public today, it doesn't take long before you see the "electronic babysitter" being used. I get it, and I've done it. Sometimes it's easier to shove the babysitter in front of their face to get something done. With the amount of travel I do, now and then I like to observe people's behavior to pass the time. Next time you're out, count how many times a child says "Mom" or "Dad" before the parent looks up from their phone and finally acknowledges their child. What message does this send to our children? I'll tell you exactly what message it sends: you are not as important as this little device made of metal and glass.

There is a time for the phone and a time to be alone. But, when you are present, be truly present and make them the most important thing at that time. Life doesn't slow down, it only gets busier. With all the responsibilities we have, where do we carve out more time for the kids? You may be working two jobs right now to make ends meet, or you may be a single parent. I get it, and God bless you for stepping up to the plate. If your time is limited, concentrate on making the time you do have with your kids as focused as possible. It may be necessary to focus on the quality versus quantity, depending on your situation.

Say Yes to Saying No

As dads, our primary job is to parent our children, not to be their best friend. Friendship can and often does come later in life, once they have reached adulthood. One of the keys to remember here is that it is our job to set the expectation, not control the child's response to it. Kids can be master manipulators and overpromise future results to get what they want in the moment. Combine this with dads who have good intentions wanting to give kids what they themselves didn't have, and many times you end up with the child in control, not dad. Our focus needs to be long term versus short term. Much like a "nook" pacifier, if we can deal with the relatively short-term crying, screaming, and sleepless nights, there are long-term benefits, i.e., having the child done with the nook for good far outweighs giving in.

One last thing: Saying no is important at times, but shouldn't always be the first word out of your mouth. Unless there is a boundary line that requires a firm "no," it is okay to respond with a "why" question. There is great benefit in allowing kids to use their voice of reason and modeling proper listening.

Encourage Decision Making

There are two types of leaders in this world: insecure and secure. Now you're thinking, "Wait a second. Did I just wormhole into a business book?" Give me a chance and I'll explain why I think this premise of leadership fits so well here. With this principle, there are specific ways you help transition leaders from insecure to secure. The overriding way is by giving the insecure leader small successes.

This is no different with our kids. By giving them the chance to talk through and experience possible actions and consequences, we give them the opportunity for these small successes. I am constantly looking for the opportunity for my boys to make decisions. Depending on the consequences, we may talk through the options together, or I may leave it up to them entirely. The expectation is, they will deal with the conse-quences of their decisions.

In our school district, once the kids reach fifth grade they have an "agenda booklet" they must fill out each day, listing what they did in school and homework yet to do. For filling it out completely and getting their parents' signature, they get points toward a class celebration. I made my expectation clear, I would not sign the agenda unless they first did the work required of them. After missing one or two of these celebrations, they fully understood how their decisions had consequences in the real world. These and small successes in other areas have helped direct their thought process in a positive way.

A Kid's Video Camera Is Always on Record

Roughly five years ago we made the three-and-a-half-hour trip down to Storden, Minnesota, (population 219) to celebrate my grandmother's ninety-seventh birthday. Before I completely embarrass and humble myself on this one, you need a little backstory. Our youngest, Everett, is my shop buddy. If I am outside, he is right there beside me. It doesn't matter what I am doing, if I don't have two of whatever I am using, he finds a stick and that's his tool. When I'm lying on a creeper under a vehicle changing oil, he's right there on his own creeper. Wrenches in hand, fixing whatever needs it, or doesn't. At eight years old, he helps rebuild the carbs on his dirt bike and knows the terminology as well.

Back to the story. Almost everyone on my mother's side of the family is at the birthday party. It is a celebration of one of the most conservative, well-mannered, churchgoing women of God I know. Trust me, there is a reason for that description. At this stage of the game, Everett is talking. However, not everything comes out clearly. Except this time…ohh no…this time was clear as a bell. Standing in the middle of the room, he began to swing his arms and sing a song—well, not the whole song, but enough of it. The song was "The B!@# Came Back" by Theory of a Deadman. I almost swallowed my tongue. Brenda immediately shot me "the look," and all I could do was mouth, "I'm sorry." We are able to laugh about it now, and yes, the radio in my shop has since been tuned to country stations only. (Come to think of it, I'm not sure if that's really much better.)

The point is, I learned quickly how they are never on pause and always on record. In leadership, you are taught the higher you go on the ladder of leadership, the more people are watching. It is no different with kids…they are always watching and repeating. We need to be modeling the right behaviors and actions for their camera. If we don't treat our wife with respect, our daughters will think that's how they will and should be treated. Just as bad, our sons will grow up to think that is how you treat a woman. If we don't stand together with our wives in decisions, especially about the kids, they will quickly understand the power of divide and conquer, making one or both of your lives a nightmare. If we model love, understanding, and firm but fair discipline, it's a good chance those will be repeated as well.

Let's not forget something as simple as manners and respect. Why are manners important, other than they are (or used to be) the social expectation? If you look to the future, good manners could influence opportunities such as employment, financing, dating, and more. When it comes to respect, there is something I have talked at length with our boys on. It is the difference between a sheep, a wolf, and a sheepdog. If you ask our boys which one they are, they will tell you without hesitation, "we are sheepdogs." Initially I thought this was good for boys to learn, but after some recent field trips, it might be a good idea for some girls to learn too. A sheep is an animal that relies on others or the herd for protection, and because of this, the old saying "get one to go and they all will go" is absolutely true. A wolf is a predator, an animal that naturally preys on others. A sheepdog is friendly, loyal, and protective in nature, looking out for those who can't look out for themselves. It is a great analogy kids can grasp the meaning of, even as young as five, six, or seven years old.

Play for Fun and Be an Imagination Engineer

To this day, fun for me is starting some kind of new project I get to build with my hands. And if I'm really lucky, I get to do it alongside my own dad. The hardest part is finding myself taking the lead in these projects instead of learning from him. But, that is a story for another book.

I have to make a conscious effort to play just for fun. I am grateful to Brenda for her influence and reminders. That accountability is helping me change slowly. By the time the boys graduate from high school, I might just have a handle on it. Lately, I've been reflecting on the time period I grew up in. During summers it was different years ago. Ball fields were full of kids pretending to be Nolan Ryan or George Brett. Playgrounds were not just swings and platforms but integral pieces of the *Millennium Falcon* or X-wing fighters. This was much more than simple fun and free time. It taught conflict solving—you piss off the guy who brought the ball or bats and the game was over, so you had to learn how to get along with others. You learned the art of relationships, problem solving, and unleashing your imagination. Most importantly, no adult was there to tell you the possibility of becoming a professional baseball player was a long shot, or your ideas were ridiculous. Today, everything from a young age is ruled by adults, figured out *for* kids, and rigidly structured. I want to scream sometimes….For cryin' out loud they're not miniature adults, they're kids. Why can't we just let kids enjoy those few short years where they get to play and run just for the sake of the fun?

Laugh Long and Hard

If I had a dollar for every time over the last thirteen years I have heard, "In twenty years you'll miss these days," I'd have another great retirement fund. Typically, this advice comes from someone whose kids have already left home and, oddly enough, has more wisdom than you do. With three boys, all two or less years apart from each other, you can only begin to imagine what we have to laugh or cry at. I'm going to tell you one of those stories and it will most likely result in me having to pay my oldest a handsome sum for the embarrassment I am about to unleash. I love ya, bud, but it's too funny not to tell.

Roughly eight to nine years ago, we suffered some serious storm damage on our previous house. Since I am kind of handy, it ended up being more of a blessing than anything. We were able to replace all of the siding, roof, windows, and doors for the cost of the damages. One morning my dad, brother-in-law, my friend Randy, and I were at the front of the house, finishing cedar tongue and groove on the ceiling of the covered porch. All of a sudden from the back deck, Brenda yells, "*Scott Charles Schuler!*" All husbands know the yell I'm talking about. It wasn't one of love and adoration, or even hurry, come here, something's wrong. Nope, this was the one of pure irritation and annoyance. As I looked at the others guys standing there, each one of them had the look of, "Glad it's you and not me, dude." I thought to myself, it's way too early for me to have screwed something up already.

When I found her at the back of the house, I asked the obvious question, "What did I do?" Her response was, "Your son just took a crap in the backyard. Did you teach him that?" Looking back, I probably could have thought a little more about my response. But, being a little bit of a smart aleck, I let fly with, "Finally, I've been working on that with him for months, I never thought he would catch on!" She didn't find as much humor in the comment as I did.

I should let those of you who never grew up in the country or on a farm in on a little secret though. At a very young age, farm and country boys are taught, usually by dad, that every tree in the woods is your personal urinal. The only rules are, don't let it rip if there are women around and don't pee on the electric fence. (I found out early on. I also learn better from experience than instruction.) This being said, I did not teach any of my sons it was okay to crap in the backyard, pee into the ditch waving at cars passing by, or drop their pants to the ankles and pee on the preschool playground. If you're like anyone else who has heard this story before, you are at the very least snickering a little. My point to this story is, as parents our kids are going to do things that at the moment we may find little humor in. I will challenge you when this happens to take a step back and see it for what it is. Don't miss a great opportunity to laugh at the situation and with them.

Wrestling 101

In the past few years, my boys have reached the age where they could sign up for organized sports. The first ones I suggested, like any good dad, were the ones I had played in high school. Unfortunately for me, they all chose wrestling. I have nothing against the sport personally, other than I have no clue how to do it correctly. I was a basketball guy, not a wrestler. But, I wasn't going to be the one who stopped them from doing something they wanted to try.

Every small town has the one sport they are known for and excel in, and wrestling is ours. In fact, at the first practice, I think 90 percent of the dads whose kids were there went to and wrestled for that school. Although I didn't know much about it, I quickly realized it didn't matter how big they were, the little one with better technique was still killing them. At one point, each of their eyes met mine with the look of, "Help me, Dad, what do I do?" My only thought was, "I don't know, ask *his* dad!"

They have since lost interest in wrestling, but one thing hasn't changed: they love to wrestle with dad. Usually this involves three against one, which by the way used to be easy. Not so much anymore. For boys, physical affection with our fathers can be a fondly remembered thing. Neil Chethik, in his article "What Sons Need from Their Dads," sums this up best when he writes, "Physical contact between a father and son gives the son a close-up view of the beast he will one day become: a man. The boy experiences, in his body and bones, how a man moves, feels, smells. Just as importantly, when the father's touch is playful and loving, the son learns that men are strong, but that strength can be harnessed, restrained, and used in a safe way."

Taking the time to do something this simple has an incredible bonding impact. It doesn't matter if you know how to wrestle at all. What matters is the time and attention you are giving. Growing up, my dad made a wager with me. It was the same bet his father made with him: if I could pin him for a count of three before I reached the age of eighteen, he would buy me any car I wanted. I did buy a vehicle, but it wasn't the Ferrari I had my eyes on, and Dad has yet to be pinned for the three count. I have made the same bet with my boys. This has resulted in being ambushed on the couch watching TV, in the backyard, while working in the shop, and coming into their rooms to tuck them in. The laughter and fun we have had from this is immeasurable. It's funny though—people think the reason I work out like I do is to look good and be healthy. In reality, there is an ulterior motive: I'm scared if I don't. There is a good chance I'll end up buying a Lamborghini, Porsche, and monster truck for sixteen-year-old boys.

Why did I make this bet with my boys? The answer is quite simple. It is the same reason for many of the other things I do with my boys. I certainly didn't realize it at the time, but those very things with so much meaning that dad took the time to do with me are the things I am trying to repeat with my boys. What things did your dad do with you? If you didn't have a dad like that, what things would you want your sons to remember? It's up to you to create that moving forward. MAN UP and break the cycle. How much do our actions as dads play a part in the development of our sons/kids?

Still on the fence for the need to MAN UP as a dad? There is a story about a Catholic nun in South America who worked in a men's prison. I've looked and looked to try and verify if this story is 100 percent true or not. I could not, but I believe it's possible and I like the story, so here it is. One day a prisoner asked her to buy him a Mother's Day card for his mother. She did, and the word got out to other prisoners, and pretty soon there were more requests than she had cards for. The next day she put in a call to Hallmark Cards, which donated to the prison several large boxes of Mother's Day cards. The inmates lined up to get, fill out, and send their cards to their moms.

Since the cards were such a hit with the inmates, the nun decided to call Hallmark again to see if they would send Father's Day cards for the inmates to mail out. As Father's Day approached, the warden announced free cards were again available at the chapel. To the nun's surprise, *not a single prisoner* ever asked her for a Father's Day card. Before his passing in 2009, Irving Kristol quoted this startling fact: "Almost two-thirds of rapists, three-fourths of adolescent murderers, and three-fourths of long-term prison inmates were abandoned by their fathers." Another study revealed that 92 percent of prison inmates hated their fathers. This story and set of facts should make us think long and hard as fathers about the importance of our role in how our sons (and daughters) turn out in life.

In the thirteen short years I've had children, John Maxwell's book *Sometimes You Win, Sometimes You Learn* has become a great comfort to me. Some of my biggest victories and failures have been as a dad. But, the lessons I have and continue to learn from these failures only serve to make me better. Strive to be a dad that…makes memories, goes on great adventures, always puts his family first, makes sacrifices, is patient, always has the time for his kids, is a great teacher, loves his kids and their mother unconditionally. If you screw these up—and you will, we all will—just know this: if you do just this one thing, everything may not turn out perfect, but it's going to be okay. Ninety percent of being a good dad hinges on one thing…*showing up!*

One of the dads I know who definitely shows up was the choice to interview for this chapter, and Kevin Wilson brings some great insight and tips for being a world-class dad. Kevin has been married to his wife Annie for seventeen years and they have a boy named Ethan, who is fourteen, a twelve-year-old boy named Kaden, and a seven-year-old daughter, Jayci, who is dancing in heaven today. As Kevin says, "So that's been our storm that we faced in 2016, and we are just kind of moving through every day at a pace that we know that God is leading us at."

MAN UP as a Father: Interview with Kevin Wilson

Scott: Alright, Kev, let's get into the first question. I know you, and how bad you want to and attempt to be a good dad. When I see what you do with your boys and the experiences you gave Jayci while she was still physically with the family, you strive to be much more than a good dad. What are the top three things that you do or try to keep at the front of your mind to be that great dad?

Kevin: I have a couple things that I live by every day, whether it be at home or at work. My main mission in life is to motivate, inspire, and encourage people consistently on a daily basis. When it comes to my family and when it comes to raising children, it's all the more. So I would say that the top three things that I keep at the very top of my mind every day is going to be I want to motivate, encourage, and inspire my boys in their faith. That's going to be number one for us. The way that I do that, I try to get a little bit creative every single year because it adds some of the memory aspect that they will take on with them when they leave our home.

For instance, last year in 2016, we got these regular dice, and we had six different "I am" statements that we would say in our household. In fact we still use them into 2017, but this was mainly the 2016 focus. So we would roll the dice in the morning before they went to school or before they went out to do whatever they were going to do in summer, and the number that it landed on represented an "I am" statement. For instance, if it was (1) I am deeply loved, (2) I am highly favored, etc., and that "I am" statement was what we carried on throughout the entire day to keep it at the top of our mind.

In 2017, the theme of the year is "Jesus is ____," and we have to fill in that blank. Every day, before the boys go to school, I ask them, "Jesus is what to you this morning?" and they'll fill in the blank, and then I'll fill in the blank, and then the story that kind of parallels with this and the whole drive behind the Jesus is blank concept is I talked with them the other day, and I said, "You guys heard of Tom Brady, right?" Well, of course they've heard of Tom Brady. "Dad, he's the greatest NFL quarterback in history." "Have you ever met Tom Brady?" "No, we haven't met Tom Brady." "Do you know Tom Brady?" "No, we don't know Tom Brady." And my biggest thing as a dad is that I don't want my boys just to hear about Jesus and never have met him or know him, and so that's the entire thing with the

Jesus is blank concept. I want Jesus to be at the top of their mind all year in 2017 and beyond obviously, but those are just some creative things that we do on a daily basis to keep their faith at the top level.

The second thing that I try to do, and this is an ongoing growing thing for myself, is voice that I respect them and tell them that I am proud of them and that I honor them. That is probably one of the biggest things as a man when you look at the needs of men and when you look at your boys. They're not just boys. They're young men. When they start off and they're going through their adolescence, they're still little men. They carry those traits that they want to be honored and respected. I wrote down that one of the deepest needs of a man is the desire to be respected and honored. That is literally one of the deepest needs a man has. If you look at what men do for honor and respect, they go crazy for the stuff. Why do young men at eighteen years old go and join the military? It's because they have a desire to be honored and respected. And why do they do the things while they're in the military that are beyond anything that I would have imagined doing in my own life? Why did they do those things? Why do they jump out of planes? Why do they go on these missions? It's because they want honor and respect so bad that they are willing to die for their brothers, they're willing to die for their leaders, and they're willing to die for their country. You want to talk about honor and respect on a whole new level, that's insane.

I just wrote a little paragraph that I'll read to you because I can't regurgitate it and blabber it off, but respect is huge when it comes to being a father to boys because it allows me to see the best in my boys. I know and have grown to understand that when I show them respect, they will put forth their best effort. It's like a switch that turns on, the ability to accomplish and fulfill something with a new determination, and when you couple that with honoring them and letting them know that you're proud, they may be only five feet three inches and five feet six inches, but they feel like giants on the inside. You inspire them to be giants on the inside, and you encourage them to be giants on the inside. Why? Because big men do big things. I desire for my boys to accomplish big things with the time that they have been given on this earth, and that's the entire reason behind why I try to voice that I honor and respect them and let them know that I'm proud of them.

That would be number two. The third thing that I keep at the top of my mind is spending time with them. When you look at the amount of time that we have, we all have twenty-four hours a day, we all have seven days a week, and we all have 52.143 weeks per year, right? Time is the greatest asset in developing a relationship with my boys. I have yet to hear a child say, "Hey, Dad, you've spent too much time playing with me. I think that you should probably go to work." They don't say that. You're never going to hear that from a child. Sometimes with the routine of life, business, jobs, and trying to focus as a dad, what we communicate to our family is "I am lacking enough time to give you what you want and need."

One of my ultimate goals is to share two of their interests with each of my sons. My twelve-year-old loves video gaming, and there needs to be times that I go in there, sit, and game even though I'm absolutely horrible at gaming. I will most likely get my butt kicked every time, but just being there side by side with another man who is my son builds that relationship. Kaden also really likes it when you listen to him when he is actually communicating something that he feels is important or when he is showing you that thing. For instance, he was posting a YouTube video the other day on his gaming, and he is like, "Dad, you've got to come in and look at this." Well, rather than being like, "Hey, just a minute," I rushed in there to show him he was top priority.

With Ethan, I went and tried snowboarding. Well, it's awful if you watch me because I spend way more time on my butt than actually going down the hill, but Ethan and his friends get a really good kick out of it and a really good time just watching it and laughing at me and making fun of me. At the end of the day, he really appreciated it. There was Dad coming out and actually spending time with us, being with us and enjoying our time together. The second thing with Ethan is he loves people, and so whenever he has friends over or whenever we're out in public, being with him with his friends and seeing the interaction there and the interaction between his friends and me, they just all love it. If I don't focus on these every week, time will fly by, and some day there is going to be a time when the house is quiet, and I will long for the times that the house was loud and active.

"Spend time with the ones you love. One of these days, you will either say I wish I had or I'm glad I did." I absolutely love this quote by Zig Ziglar. That's kind of a thing that helps keep all that pulled together and all in one basket.

Scott: I remember, one time you told the story. I don't remember if it was Ethan or Kaden, about how you went into his room. He was playing a video game or something, but you just sat there. You didn't say anything. You just sat there and watched him, and his comment later to you was, "Dad, hey, thanks for spending time with me." And you did absolutely nothing other than just sit there. And that struck me as like, man, how important is just the presence? I mean, true presence, where there's nothing else going on, there are no other distractions that are taking our time away, and you're just present? They notice it, and they notice when we're distracted.

Kevin: It's so true…just our dedicated presence as fathers is powerful.

Scott: I had to ask this question because whenever we're together, we're laughing, and for me, humor is important and if I'm not having fun and I'm not laughing, then there's something wrong.

There really isn't anything that I shouldn't be able to laugh at unless something unfortunate has happened to someone. And even then, sometimes I'm a little irreverent. I haven't been struck by lightning yet....How important is a sense of humor when raising kids and especially boys?

Kevin: It should be mandated by law that if you have boys, there has to be a sense of humor involved in the household. That's how important that is. The thing that I have noticed, they think up the funniest stuff that they think is hilarious, and a lot of it really has to do with anything that starts with the letter P. The things they think of and come up with are so funny. Whether it's poop, puberty, or pee, you need to put a bright spin on it, you know what I mean? If you don't continually put that sense of humor in and you grow with them, we can become these fathers that are a little uptight and maybe have some unrealistic expectations for our child to act a certain way.

There is a danger that comes into play here. It has to do with the things that they want to share with you and have shared with you in the past. As they read your reaction and if it's not the right reaction, they can eventually start to get to the point where they are not going to share those things with you anymore. As a father, I want to be a moments father. What you do is you capture these moments with your kids as if they were recorded with a video camera or as if someone was actually watching you. You're capturing these moments so that when they bring up a certain topic, the moment there needs to be something that is going to be extremely intimate between a father and a son, and it's something that we can replay in our minds over and over and over again, and they can replay in their minds over and over again to where they say, "You know what? I know that Dad thought that this was what it was when I was telling him about this topic. I feel comfortable with talking to him about this topic in the future." And what they do is they continually play on those moments, and they never forget those moments.

Those things are like word picture in our minds, and it makes it easier to go back over those moments with our fathers. Some of the greatest conversations that I had with my dad growing up were when we were out knee deep in a lake throwing lines in the water catching fish. We would sit there talking and I would throw something off color to Dad, who was always a little bit more conservative than I was. We had a lot of laughs and moments from the answers that he would try to manufacture on the spot. Later on, he would come back and say, "Hey, I want to just add to that conversation," when in fact what I know what he was doing was, "I have no idea how to deal with this right now, but...here's what we're going to do." It's those moments we remember for life.

Scott: It's almost like as we become men we lose the ability or the willingness to laugh at something just to laugh...it just leaves. I've lost track of the number of nights eating out somewhere, it has turned into a Beavis and Butthead episode. The boys start laughing and I look at them like, "Really?" After I start thinking about it, pretty soon I'm laughing, and it's like you said, one of those moments you just don't forget. I may have to explain what that is for those under the age of thirty-five reading the book.

Kevin: "I'm the Great Cornholio."

Scott: You and I still have things to learn, as fathers of new teens and younger. We still have memories to create and moments that may surpass other moments that we've already had. But in raising your boys, so far, what's been your biggest success or moment of like, "Wow, hey! I did a pretty good job there?"

Kevin: Can I say, conceiving them?

Scott: Well I guess for some that is a significant achievement, so sure.

Kevin: You're too generous...I would say honestly the biggest success that I have right now is I know beyond a shadow of a doubt, my boys love me and they are not embarrassed of me. I'll take that as a huge win, considering what I see everywhere else.

When it comes to like a crushing success, it's so hard to think back because there are things that I know that made me super proud. When Ethan started playing football, he had just this, it's this natural thing because it definitely did not come from me. But to be the father and be like, "Yeah, you know, that was...I'm involved in a family, it's probably from my wife's side that gave him all that talent," but able to take that credit, I feel really good. Being proud of watching their accomplishments on a daily basis is just a success, and I would say that as of right now the biggest thing is that no matter what they're doing in life, no matter what they accomplish and no matter what goals they go after, as long as at the end of the day they love Jesus and they're going to be spending eternity in Heaven, I feel like that will be a crushing success.

Scott: As you look back as a dad, which ones stand out like, "Man, I wish I could have that one back?"

Kevin: I would say that the biggest one that I wish I could have back was when I was working a job that kept me away from home and in different states. I was completely missing out on the moments back here at home, and at the time, I thought it was a good idea. Losing Jayci woke me up and really put a lot of this stuff into perspective, like where all that time really mattered. If I had to do it all over again, I would adjust my work to where I wouldn't have been working that far from home. There's nothing better than being able to walk through the door and seeing your family in operation. To see the family unit that creates all these different dynamics on a daily basis puts a huge smile on my face. It's the best feeling in the whole world, and so I wish

MAN UP AS A FATHER

that I would have readjusted my life then to really bring it back to where I was needed and where I belonged.

Scott: That focus piece.

Kevin: Focus, that's what it is.

Scott: When you look at discipline, because hopefully we all discipline our kids. With discipline and praise, is it directed toward the person or the character? I want your thoughts on that.

Kevin: That question is just loaded.

Scott: I'm not nice, am I?

Kevin: When I saw the first three text messages come over, I was like, oh yeah, yeah, this will be alright. And then I start seeing these next couple questions and I'm like, what is he doing to me? He chose the wrong guy.

Scott: No, I really didn't.

Kevin: So I think that when it comes to discipline and praise and then person and character, I almost have to talk about discipline a little bit and about praise a little bit to bring it to that level.

Scott: Perfect, because that's what I wanted you to do.

Kevin: First and foremost, I believe that discipline is absolutely 100 percent necessary. I think that if it's something that if you claim that you are a father who genuinely cares about your children, discipline is going to rear its head over and over again, because that's where teaching, training, and coaching moments come from. They are the things we carry on through the rest of our lives as we aspire to find mentors that will teach, train, and coach us and actually discipline and bring discipline to our lives as well. What does that have to do with character? Well, when you discipline correctly, character grows. That's one of the biggest things. If you look at some of the ways that I have disciplined in the past, I have disciplined to the point of actually kind of

125

degrading my boys on really who they are as people because I wasn't thinking through it. I was disciplining in the heat of the moment and I didn't take time to pull back and process before I actually could teach properly. It needs to be clear and not blurry when you discipline. That's the biggest thing.

Scott: So are you disciplining the character that they exhibited or who they are as a person? There's that fine line of I'm going to discipline the character that they displayed, not who they are as a person, because I don't want to injure or harm their spirit.

Kevin: Exactly. How do they say it? You can shear a sheep as many times as you want to, but you'll only cut them once. This resonates completely with discipline. When you start cutting deep, they remember those things. It's tough to take back, and here's the key that I've learned in my own parenting of fourteen years. There are times when it is absolutely 100 percent necessary to go to your child after disciplining them improperly and saying, "I'm sorry. Will you forgive me?" That is one of the toughest things as a father to do on planet Earth. In general, I think as a parent, even for a mom, it's one of those things that we think that we should have figured out by now, and actually it's being brought to the table. That's tough, bro.

Scott: It is, but I think it's one of the most powerful teaching moments for our boys, our kids, that we can give them too.

Kevin: That's right.

Scott: Yeah, it's tough. That's a big dose of crow there.

Kevin: That's a big dose of crow. The other side of it is when you discipline properly and all of a sudden sometimes they regurgitate or model that behavior back to you...that's even more humbling.

Scott: The student has now become the teacher. Yeah, I've already had that. It sucks from a five-year-old.

Kevin: Yeah, the five-year-old's got ya. So yeah, I think that discipline can be, I think that it's necessary to grow, but you gotta do it where it's clear and not blurry.

Now let's talk about praise a little bit. Praise can be like candy to a child. A little bit is okay, but when they need it over and over and over again, that's where some pretty rough things can happen in their lives to where they actually have to live their lives by the praise of others, and then what happens with that is they don't realize that life is beyond who they are and beyond what they did and beyond what people are saying about them because you start to live in that praise mentality, and now it comes down to what others think about you constantly and not developing who you are. When you look at praise, I think the main thing to do with praise is to turn it more into encouragement. I think that that's the fine line. Praise says, "You got an A, there is no one smarter than you," right? Encouragement says, "Congrats. You worked hard. You deserve it." There's two different things there. And I think that when we encourage our kids and our children and we consistently bring in that piece that the reason why you are able to be praised is because of the work that you put in behind the scenes to accomplish that mission and that goal. That's the huge divider.

Scott: That's that character piece again.

Kevin: That's right.

Scott: It's the whole "because of this, you accomplished that." With the key being them learning how there's good consequences and bad consequences, depending on what you did. Let's move on and get your opinion on the word "no" and participation trophies. Are you a participation trophy dad, Kevin?

Kevin: I'm not.

Scott: No?

Kevin: I know it's hard to believe. But here's the thing. Do I wanna be? Yeah, but if we jump into it, we're going to learn that participation trophies are something that is really hindering their growth in the future. I think the trophies should be awarded to winners, the first, second, and third place people, right? For instance, guys like Anderson Silva and Georges St-Pierre of the MMA. They deserve a trophy, you know? You've got people like LeBron James, Michael Jordan, and Stephen Curry. They deserve a trophy. Jordan Spieth, Jason Day, and Tiger Woods in the PGA, they deserve a trophy. Winning teams like the New England Patriots also deserve trophy, but the reason why they deserve a winning trophy is because those guys and teams have put so much blood, sweat, and tears into working on that element of who they are and their game. The trophy is the acknowledgement for putting the blood, sweat, and tears into this to make it the best, so that others can appreciate it, and maybe strive to be better themselves. Now, if you're giving trophies to everyone for just participating, what you're really doing is you're lowering the overall value and performance of everyone else who has worked their keister off to do that, and it becomes this thing of, "I'm entitled to it because _____." In real life that gets you nothing.

Scott: Right. Can you see me going into the MMA ring and going, "Hey, I'm here. I'm not gonna fight, but I want a trophy just because I stepped into the ring, so give me my trophy and I'm good."

Kevin: That's right. Please, just give it to me. I deserve this.

Scott: What do you mean? I showed up.

Kevin: Right? So yeah, participation trophies, yeah, I don't like that. Now when it comes to the word "no," I think that the word "no" is something that we do need to use, especially when it comes to raising children, but again, it comes down to some of these creative ways that we can use the word "no" because I'm used to growing up in my family from a different generation of fathers that my dad said, "No," and then I'd be like, "But Dad, why?" and he'd say, "Because I am your father."

Scott: The "because I said so" rationale?

Kevin: Exactly! Even though that was one way of doing it, it left a lot of questions inside of who I was and the decisions that I thought that I needed to make, and it was not necessarily setting me up for success. When you say no, I think that it can be packaged in a way that it can be a learning experience. For instance, "I don't think that you should do that. Do you think it's wise?" And always following up with a question after saying no, because they'll start to answer that question themselves. When they make the right decision, they get the feeling inside you can't really explain, where you feel good about what you did, knowing you made the right choice.

One of the things that I can reference right now is a couple summers ago, Ethan and his friends wanted to go ding-dong ditching. They had actually gone ding-dong ditching about a week before this particular weekend came up. I told them, I said, "Ethan, I just want to let you know that some people don't view life through the same lens that you do, and some people don't necessarily appreciate ding-dong ditching. In fact, some people might go as far as even possibly pulling a gun and shooting at you. Do you think that it's wise to do that?" We sat around and chitchatted for just a little bit, and he called his friends and just said, "Hey, guys. I'm not gonna go ding-dong ditching." Well, anyways, his friends had still gone out, and lo and behold, the cops got involved, and it was the night that Ethan had decided I'm not going ding-dong ditching. Not only was it confirmation that he had made the right choice, but we had the opportunity to affirm him for making the right choice since we were involved in the decision-making process. When you have those two things playing into each other, it works really well.

Instead of just saying no, talking it out as a family and following up with a question can be highly beneficial.

Scott: This leads us right into the next question. Let's talk about the helicopter or the hovering parent versus encouraging your kids to achieve independence to take risks, that piece of not mothering them to death. Nothing wrong, mothers are a great thing. I love my mother. I'm sure you loved your mother and still love your mother, and mothers serve an incredible purpose in a boy's life. I really believe for boys, that risk-taking piece is hardwired into us. We're going to build a ramp, and we're going to jump our bikes over it. We're going to climb up a tree, tie a rope to the highest branch we can, and we're going to swing from it. It doesn't matter if that branch is dead or alive or that rope is cut or broken and it's gonna break. We're gonna do it because it's what we're wired to do. My question is, how do you balance that?

Kevin: Here's the thing, I think, when it comes to the helicoptering versus some of the "go get 'em" risk taking. I heard a story a long time ago that I honestly don't know if this is true or factual, but I like the entire premise behind the story, and the only reason I don't know if it's true is because I've never gone out and actually observed the habitat of a bald eagle, but I know that when you're driving down the road and you see a bald eagle, it's attention grabbing, right? It's a bird that you're like, "That is an amazing bird," you know?

So I heard a story a long time ago that goes something like this. There was a mother bald eagle that came home to her nest without food, and all of the baby bald eagles were looking at her saying, "Where's our food, Mom?" She hovered over the nest at about three feet and was doing that so that they would see that the little things on the back of their backs actually serve a purpose. She came down, swooped into the nest, and started nudging baby bald eagles toward the edge. She got them closer and closer until she eventually pushed one baby out of the nest.

The baby bird tumbled and twirled all the way to the ground, freaking out because it thought that it was gonna hit the ground and die. However, just at the last second, she swooped down, caught the baby bald eagle on the back of her back, and brought it up to the nest. The baby bald eagle looks at her and says, "Well, that must have been an accident." Well, then she started pushing it again and did the same thing over and over and over and over again. Eventually through the hopping around in the nest and the momma bald eagle tearing apart the house making it less and less comfortable for them to come back up and sit there and snuggle in, the baby bald eagle looks at the world and says, "I better fly; otherwise, I'm screwed."

So the point of it is I don't think that helicoptering necessarily works for the entire life span of the babies, of the children. I think that yes, there's a time that we need to make sure that we protect them, that we serve them, that we feed them, but then there's also a time where your protection goes to a push, and I think at that point in time is that moment of teaching them that the skills and the things that they've learned now, they need to apply it to their own life; otherwise, truth be told, they're going to be screwed.

Scott: If you're okay with this, and you need to tell me if you are and be honest with me if you aren't. You've alluded a little bit to what happened with Jayci this last year, and I think that is a piece of parenting for a lot of parents, and many times we try not to talk about it. It may not be the same piece and the same exact situation, but I think there is that piece in there, and I think as dads, I think your story and how you got through it could add, what's the word I'm looking for? Confidence or encouragement and how in the world to get through something like that. If you're willing to go into it a little bit, that's awesome. If you're not, dude, no pressure, none whatsoever.

Kevin: No, it's good. I think that one thing that we're continually learning is how to still process through it all. But there are a few key things that really played into kind of the entire situation even from birth. I could probably pick up at the time that we found out that Jayci was gonna be born possibly with, well, what happened was there was low fluid in the amniotic sac. It was kind of weird, we were kinda freakin' out and kinda stressin' out about that for a while, and then she was born, and we didn't really think a whole lot about it because it seemed at that point in time she's a baby, you know, things are normal, and then when we found out that she had this diagnosis, it was one of those things that at that point in time we could have decided that we were going to freak out and lose our marbles completely or we were going to view this as an opportunity to embrace what we believe is the biggest gift that God's ever given us on this earth, and we chose to go that route, because there was something about Jayci that when you were around her, the love that flowed out of her was unbelievable. Even though she had muscular dystrophy and she was bound to a wheelchair, her sassiness and her attitude and her every single day method of operation revolved around love, and she showed that with the way that she communicated with her brothers. She showed that with the way that she communicated to her friends.

One of my favorite pictures I've seen with her was when she was in school, and with one hand she was holding one friend's hand, and with the other hand, she was holding the other friend's hand. I look at that, and I view that as a sobering moment for myself because to have that kind of love that when you're around your friends, you want to hang so closely to both of them, and you want to embrace both of them with the same passion and the same compassion, it's unbelievable. It led me into studying compassion, and there's a Greek word for compassion, it's *splagchnizomai*. It's a word that describes how Jesus felt when he walked by a beggar, and he walked by and he had so much compassion that he had to stop. It's not that he could have stopped, it's not that he could have kept walking. The option wasn't there. It actually stopped him in his tracks, and so the compassion that Jayci had and the love that she had was this splagchnizomai. It was like a gut-wrenching thing.

We've learned now that that's what she functioned with. It was the fact that she wanted to enjoy life so much that she drew you in. Whether we were in Target or whether we were at therapy, the people that worked with Jayci were drawn in. As a dad and as a mom and even just a person, that's the kind of love and that's the kind of compassion that I strive to have. The fact that it's this constant drawing onto something that is greater than yourself, and that's love and compassion. It's not that people saw Jayci and were like, "Oh, she's so great." It's not her words that she spoke, it was what they felt. I'm convinced now that one of the main reasons why Jesus gave her to our family was to capitalize on some of the truths that we've built but to move forward with a determination to become that Christlike, it's just not normal. The love and compassion that she gave people, it just wasn't normal, but that's what they noticed.

Scott: One of the reasons that I chose you for this interview for the "MAN UP as a Father" chapter was because of the ways…It's funny, because what you just said, it wasn't what she said. It was what she exuded. I didn't choose you for the words that you say. I didn't choose you for your flowery language and YouTube videos and that type of thing. The reason I chose to interview you for this piece was your actions that you do for and with your kids. I look at Jayci and what you guys did with the motorcycle and the fan. Was it a fan or a hair dryer?

Kevin: It was actually a leaf blower.

Scott: Leaf blower, that's what it was. So you guys strapped her to the motorcycle and took a leaf blower so she could feel the wind on her face like she was riding the motorcycle, but there wasn't anything that, if she wanted to experience it, you were going to do your dangedest to make sure that she had a chance to experience it, and I see that the same way with your boys too, that your priority is them, and you model that piece of what Jayci exuded, it's because of what you guys model. I think for dads to strive for that piece, we're never gonna attain perfection, but to strive for that, you make the rest of us look like idiots. Thanks, man.

Kevin: That's not true.

Scott: But it's good, and that is the reason I picked, I wanted to interview you for this, because I just don't, I don't see many people who do that.

Kevin: You asked the question on how we got through it. It was more of the background leading into that. The main way that we got through it comes down to nothing but understanding the love of Jesus Christ in our lives, right? That's how we got through it. That was the driving factor, but here's the thing. There were some steps that we had to take as a family. You stay together when storms come. You don't separate. When you're together, you can accomplish more. You can set sail in the right direction with teamwork, and I think that one of the ways that we got through it was a family, number one, that they bond together so easily when something like this happens when a storm comes. We're blessed with incredible parents, we're blessed with incredible family here in Becker. And everyone came together. Powerful things happen when people come together. That's one way.

The other thing was keeping our family unit strong and centered on the focus of the life that we did give Jayci. Like you said, it's the fact that we didn't want her to miss out on life. We wanted her to embrace life with this thing called muscular dystrophy, and it was a main driver every day to make sure that we did that. It really was. When you met Jayci, you're like she just, out of everyone in our family, she's the biggest risk taker. It had to be her. And I think that now moving through it there are days that feel more like a nightmare than a dream, and you can be haunted by the events of the night that she passed on or even be haunted by what you should have done better and what you should have done greater, but if there's one thing that I've realized about the should haves is that a lot of those are just made up in your mind anyways, and you really need to focus on what you did because that's gonna cause you to be better with what you're gonna do in the future. It's a constant grind making sure that you stay focused on what you do with it now that's gonna make a difference, not only for your own family but others around you, and it's this constant outpouring and thinking through what can I do for other people, because Jayci would want us to do everything that we possibly could for everyone else.

One of the biggest things that gives me peace is that here on earth Jayci had a disability where so many people were like, "Oh, well she can't do this and she can't do that" or whatever. Well, she's in heaven now, and the thing that I keep on coming back to is, "Now who has the disability?" She's doing things that I can't do. Someday, we're gonna be able to do that, and so...

It's a rough ride, and we could go on and on, really we could. We could talk about the fruits of the spirit that we saw that came out of her, and we could talk about the different things that she accomplished by using the limited resources that she had, and we could talk about the hand that she had been dealt, but she won with it, and we could go on and on and on and on. But I think the biggest thing is just keeping some of these principles in mind that it's all about other people. It's all about learning the compassion of love, and it's all about making sure that you're pouring out constantly and learning from it. Some of that, I don't know how long you want that book to be.

Scott: No, I think what you said is exactly what people need to hear. And there will be, there's gonna be a sequel to this book!

CHAPTER 7

MAN UP SPIRITUALLY

I'm not a huge George Michael fan but he was right about this—you gotta have faith. And the truth is, we all have faith in something. You have faith that when you turn your car on in the morning that it will start. You have faith in a motorcar company run by people you've never seen. You had faith in the chair you're on before you sat down on it. (Assuming you are sitting.) Manning up spiritually means evaluating what or who your faith is in and why. It's being open to make changes to your life based on what you believe. If you are solid on what you believe, the MAN UP question then becomes: Are you living authentically and according to your beliefs? If you aren't living according to the beliefs you profess, there's a good chance you don't really believe them. How did you arrive at your belief system? Is it something your parents instilled in you? Was it something your wife chose for you?

I actually contemplated for a second about whether or not I wanted to put this chapter in the book. Matters of faith and spirituality can be so deeply personal and controversial. We've gotten along so well up to this point I certainly don't want to start something. (Don't worry, there isn't a chapter on politics.) But, at the end of the day faith is an important piece of who I am, and influences me as a man on a daily basis. My convictions keep me making right choices. My faith empowers me when I feel week. And I'm grateful. Not only that, the beauty of writing a book is that it's my dang book, so I can write whatever I want in it!

On the other hand, if this information is not your cup of tea, well you are the one reading this book and you have the power to skip this chapter if you'd like. But remember, part of manning up is being willing to explore this area and not shy away from what might be a different viewpoint than yours. (Yes...I just dared you to read this chapter.) I promise that reading this chapter won't hurt, and you may very well read some things that surprise you.

Religious Fallout

As a boy, I was raised under a conservative, rigid, Baptist philosophy. (Save the eye rolls.) I'm not saying it was bad by any means, I'm simply stating a fact. My family went to church Sunday mornings, Sunday evenings, and Wednesday nights too. I was involved in Sunday school, youth group, missions, memorizing scripture, you name it—if it was church-related, I did it.

It was at the age of sixteen when all of this changed drastically. This was the year of my first prom, which was right about nine months before I became a dad for the first time. As you might imagine this wasn't the timeline my parents had in mind. You might also be able to imagine their response. Dealing with the disappointment and shame from my parents was one thing. However, the wheels came completely off the cart when I was informed that I needed to get up in front of the *entire* church on a Sunday morning and apologize for my actions. This wasn't my parent's idea as some absurd, off the wall punishment. It was the leaders of the church, in a misguided legalistic decision, who mandated it. I now know that wasn't a biblical way to handle the situation in any way, shape, or form. I don't fault Dad and Mom now for allowing it but back then, I was pissed as...insert cuss word of your choice. They were doing what they thought was right and as a sixteen-year-old boy I was forced to "man up" in front of the entire church. As I looked out over the congregation, my first thought was, "I know firsthand how many of you sitting out there judging me have, and are, doing the same if not worse than I did. And yet, *none* of you are or have been up here begging for forgiveness." I thought, "If this is what the church does, I don't want a damn thing to do with it."

My girlfriend and I gave our boy up for adoption. As hard as it was, it was the best choice for him. I was in no way, shape, or form ready to give that child what he needed from a dad. After the adoption, I left home and went to college a year early. I ran full tilt as fast as I could in the opposite direction of what I had learned over the last sixteen years of going to church. This is not the place or time to get into specifics, and most wouldn't even comprehend it. Why did I do it? I was mad, and I placed the blame for what I was going through everywhere and anywhere but where it actually belonged. What I lacked was the maturity to admit that I was the one who made the decision to do what I did. No one forced me to do anything. I needed to take responsibility for my actions and decisions.

The Aftermath

For twenty-plus years, I was an angry man. There are a few people who know exactly who I was...very few. I learned how to be a good actor around those who thought I was still a good kid. Without exaggeration, if it were not for my incredible wife, I would either be dead or in jail at this point in my life.

Once married, and our boys were on the scene, my wife wanted us to find a church to attend. The last thing I wanted in life was to subject my boys to the "wrath of the church" if they ever happened to make a mistake. We eventually started attending different churches, but unfortunately, I discovered that the crap that I experienced, the unbiblical shame and judgment, was still as blatant as ever in the churches we attended. I would go and sit in a service, mumbling to myself, not even paying attention to what was being said. I will say one thing—even though the entire time I was actively pushing God away, I know He never left me and neither did my dad and mom. I could still feel Dad like a little angel on my shoulder saying, "Do you really think that is the right thing to do?" We visited this one church, and as soon as we walked in the door, the first comment was, "What do you do for a living?" I said, "I am a chiropractor here in town." I still can hear the response: "Oh, we already have one of those here." I grabbed my wife and boys, said, "Glad you've met your quota," and we walked out.

Even as recent as seven years ago, I was still dealing internally with the failings of churches we attended. However, my view was beginning to change, ever so slowly. A man I respect greatly pulled me aside and questioned me about my resistance to church. Evidently, I wasn't hiding it as well as I thought. His simple statement still rings true in my ears: "How long are you going to let the failure of a man-run church dictate your love for God and His love for you?"

Don't get me wrong, the first time I heard this, I wasn't thinking very Christian-like words in my head. I was ready to tell him where to go and how fast to get there! Close to that time, my wife had her eye on another church. The next Sunday, we packed up the kids and went to "try out" another one. Much to my surprise, this one was different. I actually listened a little and I could feel a tinge of conviction after the sermon. Conviction that caused me to think about what I was doing or saying outside of church. There was no way I was going to let on to Brenda about that though. And of course, as always, she saw through my facade right away. Again, evidently not very good at hiding things. I was interested enough though to try this church again.

Find Your Place

It has now been seven years since that first reluctant visit. I can truthfully and happily say, we have found our church home—a place where we are loved and accepted, warts and all. In fact, I love our church. I call it the church of misfit toys. You see, church shouldn't be a place for those who are perfect believers in God. The purpose of the church is to embrace the broken, lonely, fallen, and hurting and lead them to Christ and His hope, forgiveness, and healing. Even for someone like me who went way astray, no matter what anyone has done, the church should receive them with open arms. It should be like a hospital for wounded souls—a safe place for those who are hurt, broken, and looking to heal.

Do I still realize that someday, at some point, someone in the church—even in a leadership position—may hurt me again or someone I love? Yes, I do, and I will make it my mission to help them understand in a much shorter time what it took me twenty-plus years to understand. I have answered the call to MAN UP in this area, to make sure to the best of my ability that what happened to me doesn't happen to anyone else on my watch. So much so, I have allowed myself to be put into positions of leadership within the church. Will there be that piece of me that wants to rise up and absolutely crush whoever did the hurting? If you only knew! Let me say that Moses gets an absolute hall pass from me for defending his Jewish brother. (If you don't know the story, it's in Exodus 2.)

Passion and pain reveal to us our purpose. Part of manning up means understanding that men—people—will always have the capacity to hurt and disappoint us, even those supposedly representing God. We can't put our faith in people. However, if you look past the frailty of mankind and place your faith in God, there is nothing that man can do, or that God can't heal. I am living proof of that. Remember that premise of imperfect progress? I cannot think of a better place that it holds true than in our faith. We all fall short of the glory of God. There isn't a pastor, preacher, deacon, or pope, past, present, or future, who is perfect. But, if we simply repent and accept Christ as our Savior and ask for forgiveness when we sin, He is faithful and just to forgive us and renew us.

Here's the deal though…this isn't Monopoly, and it isn't a get out of jail free card. We need to make the choice toward making imperfect progress and being better today than we were yesterday. I'm not going to discuss a long list of points on how we can man up in our faith. My first point is a familiar one—your *ego* is not your freaking *amigo*. I look at ego as <u>E</u>dging <u>G</u>od <u>O</u>ut. That is exactly what I did, and it hurt me and others around me. Let it go already!

The second and last point may confuse you, make you mad, or you may disagree completely with me. You know what, that's okay. I hope you see by now, this is coming from someone who was totally broken and found his way back, not someone who knew it all and was perfect. It certainly wasn't through my own power or by my own devices. If left up to me, and without God, I wouldn't be who I am or where I am. If this is an area you feel there is room to MAN UP, here are a few key things you can do:

Just Do It

At some point we have to acknowledge that we don't know everything and we may never have all the answers. But in the words of country singer and songwriter Lee Brice, never let your praying knees gets lazy. Even if you aren't sure what you believe, make time to explore the unknown. A prayer can be as simple as saying, "God, if you are real, show me." If you are solid in what you believe, make time to pray with your spouse and kids. There are all kinds of studies on the benefits and power of prayer but you have to man up and do it because of how it affects you and your spirituality. Prayer doesn't have to be fancy or done a certain way; talk to Him like you would a friend. Be verbally humble, grateful, and tell Him your troubles and requests. And then listen. Prayer is a conversation. Sometimes God will speak to your heart, sometimes He'll reveal Himself in nature, sometimes through what we call "coincidences." But you'll know when God is getting your attention. When you call on Him, He promises answer.

Seek God Daily

If you are driving in your car with the radio blaring, it doesn't work too well to try to have a conversation with the person next to you. You have to turn down the radio so you can communicate. In the same way, we have to turn down the noise of the world if we want to be able to hear from God. I encourage you to carve some time out of your busy schedule for prayer and reading the Bible. Not only do I need to take time to recharge spiritually, but I'm also setting an example for my children. The way I remember the importance of this or anything I want to pass down is, "My kids will only take it as serious as I do."

Teach Your Kids

Teach your kids about God. Encourage them to question and obtain a belief of their own. If they base their belief only on what their parents say they should, it's not a belief but a mandate. Talking with and encouraging questions gets them thinking now instead of later. If later in life they are challenged in their beliefs and they are not their own convictions, the likelihood of having those beliefs change is much higher.

Find the Right Church

Look for a Bible-based church where people admit they are imperfect yet trying to be better. Associating with like-minded people is as much, if not more important for your spiritual development than it is for your personal development. Remember, challenging the heart is just as important as challenging the mind. It is not if, but *when* you will stumble, and you will need encouragement from someone who will call you on behavior that may not be appropriate. I have different mentors for different areas of my life. Some overlap and others do not. The people you give permission to and are willing to speak truth into your life are invaluable to your growth.

You've probably noticed, this chapter is the shortest one so far. However, in my mind it is the most important. The difference is how deeply personal your faith is. I can't tell you what that will look like. Only you can determine the depth it will have, based on your willingness to explore, read, and seek a personal relationship with God. If you get anything from this chapter, I hope you understand that no matter what you have done, how far you have run, or even if you have never explored faith in God, He is always there with open arms to welcome you back or embrace you for the first time.

I chose the pastor of our church, Jim Vonwald, as the person to interview for crushing it, as a man, in the area of faith. This man is down to earth and admits fully how even he, as a pastor, is making imperfect progress like the rest of us.

MAN UP Spiritually: Interview with Jim Vonwald

Scott: Let's start with just a little background. How long have you been a pastor?

Jim: Since 2002, I guess I began pastoring here, so fifteen years. I did a little stint about two, two and a half years as a youth pastor back in 1985 to 1987.

Scott: When did you know that was your calling?

Jim: I sensed something when I was probably about ten years old. I sensed something in my spirit at a time with a group of other kids at a camp that there was something occupational in ministry for me, because I did not know what that was, and so I kind of pushed it to the background of my thinking. I went through my teen high school years and did not pursue it. I pursued other interests and got into college, and during my freshman year of college, it came back to me. I had a unique experience where, the best way I can describe it was, I saw people really in need of faith in their life. It was a dream or a vision or whatever you might call it, and my responsibility was to do what I could to help them in that avenue, and so, as a result, I left where I was and I went to seminary Bible college. However, I came out of that experience, still not understanding what my calling was. I never really had anybody confront me about what that meant or what my faith even meant, and I felt like my calling was to do something for God with my life and in faith, and it didn't go so well because I tried to do a whole bunch of stuff, and I just got really tired and fed up with the work, the doing, and I just couldn't work hard enough. After a couple years of that, I was very unfulfilled, and I ran from it as fast and as far as I could go.

Scott: So you weren't always on the same path?

Jim: No. My grandpa had a saying. He would say when asked how his life was going or how his day was going, he would say, "Steady by jerks." I think that my faith walk was a series of lots of ups and downs and then mostly down for probably about fifteen years until I came to the spot where through a series of lots of different circumstances…my life had pretty much blown up and my marriage had fallen apart. I was at the spot in life with God, where literally I feel like I was probably close to being agnostic. I felt like God was out there, but my idea of thought toward Him was, "Screw you, God, I'm just going to do what I want to do," and that's what I did. And that just resulted in my life blowing up.

I really got to the spot where it was a point of decision, and I knew it was a point of decision. Even though I knew it was a decision point, I didn't quite grasp how God understands us better than we understand ourselves. He knew I needed to make this choice myself and there was no way I was going to ever be forced into making a decision of faith, or submission to him. All of these circumstances left me empty, yet my life was still moving forward very fast. I was very successful in what I was doing, and all of the things around me were relatively good, but I was really empty, and the hidden things that other people didn't see, my marriage and my faith, were gone.

Realizing the emptiness, I got to the spot where I said, "God, I give up. I've tried it my own way. What's your way? What are you saying? I want to follow you." So what does that mean? For me, it meant that I needed to go all in. Like, okay, if I'm jumpin' in, I'm jumpin' in. I'm not putting my toe in the water,

I'm jumpin' all the way in. I just said, "I'm gonna jump in, and you're gonna have to guide me in what that looks like." That really is how I've ended up being a pastor or a leader now. It was that junction in life with God and the Father. I understood that God wasn't looking for me to do something for Him. He was looking for me to be someone for Him, and being somebody was somebody He had already created. I didn't need to try to meet a certain standard or be a certain person or do something special or anything like that. I needed to walk into life and truly walk into who He created me to be. That's where for the last fifteen years I've been at.

Scott: In this book, I have discussed a little bit how true power comes from giving it away. Would you say at the point when you finally reached what you call your decision point, is when you knew it was time to give it away? I had the same point in my life where, okay, I know this is the decision. This is the pivotal point for me. It's either this way or it's this way, and whichever way I'm going, I'm probably not coming back from. That's probably where my life is going to go for the rest of my life. Would you say that was almost that man up point for you where it's like, "I'm gonna man up?" and by manning up, I mean I'm giving away... I'm manning up and saying, "I'm yours."

Jim: Yes. Totally. That's a great way to describe it, and I think that there is a scripture that comes to mind that I struggled with for quite some time in this process. It's Paul saying, "When I'm weak, then you can be strong," and I needed to understand what it meant to be weak because I've learned that I can do a lot of things on my own. The harder I try to do things on my own, the more I'm relying on my own strength and not God's strength. So that whole other side of saying, "How can I still leverage the gifts, God, you've given me and yet be weak so that you can be strong?" That piece of understanding for me came about in realizing that it wasn't physical weakness, it wasn't leadership weakness, it wasn't any of those kinds of things. It was that I was to leverage all of those with the understanding that God is going to bring me to this point that I'm going to have to be able to go further, and I can't do that on my own, and that's my weakness. That's where He will step in and be strong, so in whatever it is that I'm doing, in this case pastoring, I do need to leverage and push all of the gifts and all of who I am to that spot of failure, so to speak, because that's the spot God will step in.

The manning up was probably accepting the fear of that. It meant that if God didn't step in, I was gonna fail, which I didn't want. I didn't even like the sound of that, but I knew that I needed to go to that spot because then any kind of weakness was only on my side, it wasn't on God's side, and He would show Himself strong. So that was a key part of the very early process, and the thought or the idea of manning up for me was understanding that. I'm gonna reach this point of the end of myself that I have to trust God to step in, and manning up meant that I was just going to do that anyway, and I wasn't gonna stop at that spot where I could handle everything.

Scott: If someone were wondering where to start if they wanted to explore faith further, other than the Bible what book or books would you recommend?

Jim: Andy Stanley, *The Principle of the Path* and *The DNA of Relationships*, Gary Smalley, are two great places/books to start with.

Scott: With the vast number of different translations of the Bible, what one would you recommend to start with that makes understanding easier?

Jim: I would recommend the New Living Translation. I think it's a version in more modern language and yet still keeps some of the poetry that the Bible has, that I believe is important as a part of reading it.

Scott: How important is the piece of ownership and how pride relates to it?

Jim: The acknowledging or the facing of who we are oftentimes in life is prevented, like I'm prevented to face up to who I am, because of pride. Pride has this way of me wanting to hide my failures, me wanting to hide those areas of my life that I don't want anybody to see.

Acknowledgement or owning up has two sides. I talk about the side of acknowledging success. Sometimes pride prevents us from receiving some of the, I don't know if it's accolades or praise of success. We want to push that down and want to put it down, but God brings success into our lives, and we need to acknowledge when He does that. We need to acknowledge that God is at work, that there are gifts and talents He's given us and acknowledge that and be thankful for that, and that's something that's healthy to do.

Likewise, it's healthy for us to be on the side of acknowledging when we fail, acknowledging when we've blown it, acknowledging those kinds of things in our life, and manning up to that takes on a whole bunch of different kinds of faces. One of the things that I believe is critical in the lives of our children and the lives of our family is they see us walk through failure, and they hear our story of failure and then the change that happens when God steps in, the change that happens when we surrender. Our children have heard our story, our story of a blown-up marriage and God then bringing about restoration and healing, and those kinds of things in their lives may not be from a blown-up marriage, but there may be other aspects of their lives that they need to acknowledge something, get over their pride, get over themselves so that God can step in and do some of the healing that He wants to do and some of the work that He wants to do in their lives. The piece of acknowledging that, I believe, is prevented by pride.

Unfortunately, the power of not acknowledging failures and shortcomings is something that is used in our lives against us. There is a scripture that says whatever is hidden in the darkness is going to be brought out to the light, and I believe that's what God does in our life. That's what Christ does is He brings us into the spot where when we acknowledge our failures, some of that acknowledgement needs to be not just to God, it needs to be to other people as well. Sometimes it can be a smaller group of people that we trust or that we can be accountable for, but each time we do that, the power of that failure loses its grip on our life, and manning up and a piece of manning up and becoming the man that God has called me to be is to be freed or loosened from the grip of pride, to be loosened from the grip of past failures and understanding that God is a god of the future. He's a god of the past, the present, and the future, but we live in the present, and He plans our future and gives us hope into the future.

Scott: So on that same note, where we can let go of the past and look into the future, in the book, I talk about this because of my transition from leaving the church to coming back to the church and how this church that we attend now with you as our pastor, as I call it, it's the church of the island of misfit toys or the church of misfit Christians. It seems like there isn't hardly one of us that hasn't been broken, affected, or hurt by the church or someone in the church in some way, shape, or form. When I say that to you, how does that make you feel? What do you think about that term?

Jim: I love that picture that comes to mind, and anybody that's watched the Christmas movie and has seen the Island of Misfit Toys understands how broken all of those toys were, and yet, on that island it was filled with joy and fulfillment. In the church world, unfortunately, what's happened is, and I grew up in a church where perfection was what was expected, there wasn't any room for failure or brokenness. And so you hid all of those broken areas of your life, and if any of them were revealed, you were no longer accepted as a part of the church. I've heard it said that some churches have such stringent membership requirements to be a part of the church that for certain the disciples wouldn't be able to be members, but even Jesus Himself wouldn't be welcomed there as a member, because He wouldn't match the membership standard. Unfortunately, I do feel that Jesus is not welcome in many churches because of that.

The brokenness of who we are is what I expect the church to be. It's a church of broken people who have been healed. I understand this to be the case that if you break a bone and that bone heals, that spot where it was broken is stronger than the surrounding bone around it. I think that that's the strength of being in a place where we can get healthy, where we can heal, is that we now have a strength in our lives as a misfit toy to leverage into helping somebody else, leverage into relationship, leverage into loving others, and our own brokenness becomes the tool that God uses to find that same joy and fulfillment that we see on the Island of Misfit Toys.

Church is supposed to be this place of healing. It is not supposed to be the place where only healthy people are attracted to it. Jesus said that. He said it's the sick that need the doctor, not the healthy, and sometimes we want our churches to be this place where there's only health. Like you said earlier, I believe that the church always needs to be a place that's a hospital. The hospital is for sick people, that's where sick people go, and I'm one of those sick people, and I need the church so that there's better health ahead, there's healing ahead. Statistics sometimes are this funny thing where people use statistics to talk about the failure of the church because the divorce rate's the same as in the world, pornography is the same, or promiscuous sex is just the same in the church as it is in the world. I believe that that's an indicator, if a church is healthy, and if that's what's going on in a healthy church, that means that there are sick people who are coming in who are in need of God's mending, His healing, His healing touch. When a church can be that place, it truly is the island of misfit toys or the island of misfit church attenders or whatever you might want to call it.

Scott: I love it because I've quoted you in the beginning of the part of the chapter with the hospital. The church should be the hospital. When you said that, the first time I heard you say that, it struck me and it stuck with me. The way I looked at it as I thought about that and processed through as I was writing the book is there is this opinion, even though it is a very misguided opinion, that the people in the church have it all together. Like you said, you're one of the broke…you are our pastor, for crying out loud, and you're saying you're broken, just like I am. Some feel the church should be only for believers. Well, you can still be a believer, but there are none of us that haven't fallen short of the glory of God, and I think it's important for people to understand that's truly what the church is for. It's for everybody who has fallen short, every last one of us. None of us are ever going to be perfect, and we're all going to continue to fall short or, at the very best, make imperfect progress moving forward. One of the things I tell people to look for is a church that has that mentality, not a church that thinks it's got it all figured out.

What would you say as a pastor? If somebody says, "What do I look for in a church?" Somebody who's on a different side of the country or a different part of the world that happens to read this book and says, "Okay, I want to know more." What do they look for in a church? What should be a red flag and what should be a green flag?

Jim: That's a great question. It would really be easy if there was a sign on the door, but I have experienced my share of what I would consider unhealthy churches, which are different than imperfect churches. I think imperfect churches are where we wanna be.

Just some guideposts or some signposts, I think just walking into a church, one sign of health is laughter. The place that we mourn is at the morgue. When you walk into a church and the church has a heaviness that you can feel, a weight or a somberness, I would have concerns that there isn't a spirit of joy, a spirit of fulfillment. It's not happiness, but it's something that's deeper than that. It's joy that brings out the warmth of who we are and the love of others. Every culture is going to be a little bit different in what that looks like, but laughter is a common theme, and everybody understands a smile no matter what language you speak or what nation you come from or what continent you live on. People understand a smile, and I believe that people understand when it's real.

That would be an initial piece, the intangibles of how does, how do people connect with me when I come in is going to be something that can change from culture to culture. But love and the expression of love is something that is tangible. Am I treated like a stranger? Am I treated like someone who's not wanted? Am I treated like an outsider? Or, am I treated like a guest? When we welcome somebody into our home, if we're looking to build a relationship, we treat them different than the salesman that comes in. A salesman might stand on the outside of the door and never step foot inside. Is there a welcome? Is there a warmth? That love, that peace. I think that's something that's pretty tangible right on the front end.

I believe that worship, that needs to connect us with God, and it needs to be something that we're able to worship and express ourselves in song and in singing in a way that is meaningful. Personally, I believe that anything that is taught from the pulpit, there needs to be a biblical standard of truth that guides it, that brings truth that's relevant to our life throughout the week. I've said it before. Sunday morning is not about Sunday. Sunday morning is about the rest of the week. If I go to a church on Sunday and all I get is something for Sunday and on Monday there's nothing, no residual left for me? I think maybe either that church or I missed it on that Sunday.

A fellow by the name of Dick Footh said something that really impacted my life relationally. I think as men sometimes we have this fear of building relationships. Again, statistics are dismal when it comes to men and the relationships that they have, that they truly can count as a relationship in their life. It's between one and three in a whole lifetime where there's somebody that they can connect to, and especially in the avenue of faith. Dick said, "When I walk through life, anybody that is in a relationship with me should be getting closer to Jesus all the time because I'm following Him," and I believe this. I believe that as men when we follow Jesus, anybody that follows us is on the path to following Jesus, and so we can become a leader in people's faith lives and in their walk and just by them being our friend and by being friends with them. So when we build connections and we build relationships, what we end up doing is we end up pulling people with us closer to Jesus.

Scott: In this, I don't remember what part of the book I put it in. I think it's for friendships. It's funny you say this. For men, friendships with men, one of the things I talk about is if my absence doesn't leave an impact, my presence is a joke.

Jim: That's good.

Scott: I think it speaks to exactly what Dick says and what you were saying. If my absence doesn't make an impact on you moving forward, then my presence is a joke. What I'm doing now is meaningless.

Jim: He said something else too. He said, "The highest form of affirmation we can have in a relationship is to pray for somebody." What that means is that we believe that they are important enough to take them and whatever their need is before the God of this universe, and that's how important they are in our lives.

Just gleaning some of those and trying to be aware of some of those kinds of things that really we can take with us.

I have had the chance to sit down, and I was honored to have the chance to sit down and have breakfast with him one time, and it's just like some of those things then are pieces of another person that you take with you through life, and so that kind of speaks to the same, that piece. What piece of me am I giving to somebody else for them to carry with them through the rest of their life? Am I having that kind of an impact on them, or is it something that is easily discarded?

Scott: On that whole note, I just thought of one other thing I wanted to talk about or I want you to touch on. The importance of manning up and having a male accountability partner in your faith walk. How important do you see that? I mean, obviously God is our ultimate accountability partner.

Jim: There's this piece, if we're married, there's this piece that we have a partner in life with our spouse, but I would say from my own experience and from what I've read from others, if a man doesn't have at least two accountability partners in their faith walk, they probably will fail in their faith walk. That accountability, just that knowledge that somebody else is walking through life with us, pulls us forward in those times when we feel like stopping or sitting down. Then we pull others forward, and that's what accountability does.

Unfortunately, we don't want to talk about those issues. We just want to keep them to ourselves. We don't want to talk about some of the stuff that's meaningful and the stuff that matters, but yeah, that accountability is something, and it's something that unfortunately is something that's really, really difficult to find and to follow through with.

Scott: Part of that pride thing, I think, of not manning up and allowing somebody else to see past that facade of strength that I can put forth. It's a piece where in order to do that, there's a vulnerable piece. I know it firsthand. There's going to be a time where you become vulnerable in front of another guy, and they're going to take full advantage of it, and it's going to suck and hurt, and you're going to get ticked off and resent even doing it. But, if you truly want to move forward in life and as a person, the next piece is manning up and doing it again. That's the way I look at it.

Jim: That's good. It's getting over fear, and sometimes fear is compounded when things don't quite go the way that we wanted them to go. Again, too often we live based on our past experiences and not on what needs to happen today and in the future. I find myself often doing that and have to look to say, "What do I need to do for this to change?"

CHAPTER 8

MAN UP FOR FUTURE GENERATIONS

I firmly believe we are in the midst of a pivotal time. We are rapidly losing men who possess attributes capable of making our world a better place. The next generation needs men who aren't afraid to live authentically. Men with the following attributes:

1. Men of strong minds.

Men of strong minds know what they stand for, yet are not afraid to listen to someone with a contrary viewpoint. With conscious and careful contemplation, he is steadfast enough in his own beliefs, and even though his view may not fit the mold, or mesh with popular opinion, he stands strong in his convictions.

2. Men who understand what true commitment is.

Not looking for his next conquest, a man who understands commitment looks for ways to put his wife in the place she deserves, first. A vow is a solemn promise. What good is your word if you can't keep the promises to the woman that captured your heart? This is a man, who when he offers his hand in agreement, no written contract could be more binding.

3. Men who put others before themselves.

Struggling with any of these ideas points to an issue of selfishness. No man is perfect, including me, but if you find yourself worrying more about yourself than others, you have some work to do. This does not mean we don't take care of ourselves or pursue things that make us happy. You can't give what you don't have, so taking time to go after what fills us up is still important.

4. Men who take ownership of their actions and words.

If your words or actions offend someone, apologize. This kind of man admits when he is wrong and makes it right. He understands true power comes from giving it away. When something goes wrong he doesn't blame others. Yet, at the same time, he not only holds others accountable, he's there to walk them through making it right.

5. Men who are both brave and bold.

These are men who look for the opportunity to protect and stand up for others, men or women. They aren't afraid of being chastised or portrayed as cavemen for stepping in. Their mentality is: "I would rather stand up and be wrong than not stand up at all." Men who do not hide behind their wife, but don't expect her to hide behind him either. They protect those they love when needed and watch from a distance when it is time for the ones they love to protect themselves.

6. Men of high aspirations.

This does not mean men concerned only about money. These are men who have a purpose bigger than themselves. Those who do not wait for someone else to do it or show them the way. Men who want to effect change for the sake of the ones they love and future generations. They know when their aspirations are affecting the well-being and/or interactions with the ones they love. And, they are bold enough to put the brakes on their own aspirations for the sake of the ones they love.

7. Men who find joy in the idea of hard work.

Whether it is physical labor or the labor of thinking, this type of man does not shrink from either. He is not afraid to use his brain or his muscles if needed. Knowing this, he strives to keep both in the best shape possible, embracing the suck if needed. He knows that neither makes him more of a man, but the willingness for doing what is needed defines his capability as a man.

8. Men more concerned about being a communicator than an educator.

Whether with their spouse, kids, coworkers, or employees, these men are more focused on being understood than being right or sounding smart. He also understands talking down to or dumbing it down is an insult and he respects who he is talking to more than that. He communicates with those he loves through words and actions, realizing understanding doesn't necessarily become evident through brute force.

9. Men who understand showing love and being caring does not mean you are weak.

These men love hard and strong. There is no doubt, his wife, children, friends, and family know exactly how much they are loved, both in action and in words. This type of man understands he has the power to hurt and the power to heal wounds with his love, and he gives it away freely.

10. Men who are self-reliant.

A quote from Rocky Balboa to his son states: "The world ain't all sunshine and rainbows. It's a very mean and nasty place...and I don't care how tough you are, it will beat you to your knees and keep you there permanently, if you let it." A self-reliant man understands, if he leaves it up to someone else it may never get done. It is up to him to teach the importance of being prepared and help prepare the ones he loves for life's ups and downs. He knows the best way to ensure excellence for his children and family is to teach them how to be self-reliant.

11. Men of humility.

Humble men understand, in the words of C. S. Lewis, humility is not thinking less of yourself, but thinking of yourself less. A humble man will graciously accept praise with a "thank you," but will never accept accolades for anything he has not done. He understands that respect is not given, but earned. It costs nothing, yet gives great reward.

12. Men who understand life's journey is a marathon, not a sprint.

These men are not just focused on the end result or finish line. They take the time to enjoy all the things life and family have to offer. They see the joy in their child's eye and take the time to acknowledge their accomplishments large or small, inconvenient or not.

13. Men who understand who they "hang with" makes a difference.

Simply put, if the people you are around talk more about people or events than ideas, it's time to change your circle. They are living in the past, not looking to the future. Real men understand that type of mentality lacks humility, aspiration, ownership, and commitment—all things we should be striving to achieve.

The MAN UP Litmus Test

If you want to know whether you are living your life to the best you can, with the MAN UP mentality, there is a surefire way to figure it out. Spend some dedicated quiet time over the next few weeks and write your own eulogy. What the priest, pastor, and/or loved ones are going to say about you while you are laying in that pine box at the front of the church. Now is not the time to kid yourself either; be honest with yourself. First write down not what you think they will say to a room full of people, but rather what they really may want to say but won't.

Take your time and think this through. Try to picture each person who is there and what they would be thinking or want to say. Once you are done with that, start thinking about what you would want people to say. If you need help, think about all the categories of men I've listed above, or think about the chapters in this book. What do you want your wife to say? What do you want your kids to say? What do you want the rest of your family to say? What do you want your friends to say? What do you want your coworkers to say?

Here is the best part of this exercise. If you have made it this far in reading this book and you are not in the back of an ambulance on the way to the emergency room because of a heart attack, you still are holding your pen and your book is still being written. It doesn't matter what kind of man you have been in your past. Trust me, I am living proof of that. You have the power and choice to determine what kind of man you will be remembered as. Will it be a man that settled and didn't fight, or will it be one who fought tenaciously to be the best possible version of the man that is you. You are the only you, and you don't need anyone's permission to be the man you were designed to be.

If we want the respect we desire, it is up to us and us alone to MAN UP. If we become, even if we attempt to be, the type of men in each of these chapters, there will no longer be a need to apologize for being a man.

The Power of a Declaration

A manifesto is simply a public declaration. There is something incredibly powerful about making a public declaration. It sets your intention and resolve towards a goal and when you have witnesses, you have a layer of accountability, strength, and support. You are probably familiar with one of the most famous public declarations of all, the Declaration of Independence. The Declaration of Independence was signed on July 4, 1776. That's when the American colonies declared their freedom from England and it's the reason Americans celebrate Independence Day on July 4 of every year. However, what most people don't realize is that the war to be free, the American Revolutionary War, lasted from 1775–1783, seven years past the declaration. The colonists declared their resolve and set their focus when they were only a year into battle, but they had the fortitude to ban together and press forward until they finally had victory.

Today, I'm asking you to set your resolve and make a declaration to MAN UP. You may not have arrived yet, but that's okay. Like the colonists, set your focus and intention until you see the victory. Ban together with other men and let's start a revolution. Let's be determined to stand and fight no matter how long it takes. The time to MAN UP is now. As you read the manifesto on the following pages, let the words sink down deeply into your heart. Notice there are two spaces for witnesses to sign with you. Choose whomever you'd like, a spouse, friend, loved one, pastor, or family member and read this declaration out loud. Sign the bottom and then go online to ManUpProject.com/Manifesto to join the movement. This world needs you, your family needs you, and you need you. Thank you for answering the call to MAN UP.

MAN UP MANIFESTO

I choose to MAN UP as an individual and always stay true myself. I will follow my own path and live out of the passions my heart. I will make decisions based on my own value system while also considering the impact of my choices on others. I renounce fear and choose to step out of the boundaries of my comfort zone knowing that opportunity and growth await. I will stay focused on the goals in my heart, and press past difficulties to achieve what I seek. I will not shrink back, hold back, put up, or give up.

I choose to MAN UP in the workplace. I take full responsibility for where I am in life. I will not compare my progress to others but learn from their successes and failures, as well as my own, so that I can be the best version of me possible. I will work wholeheartedly at every-thing I set my hand to and always maintain an attitude of excellence. I will pursue my passions wisely and guard my thoughts and inner circle, carefully sifting through the influences in my life. I will find the value of my "why" and let it fuel me on my path. I will persist against all odds and choose an attitude of gratitude in all things.

I choose to MAN UP in my health knowing that no one else can do this for me. I will make a conscious effort to care for my body physically and be the best I can be. I renounce excuses and make sure the story in my head will set me up for success. I will "embrace the suck" because I want to thrive in all things in life!

I choose to MAN UP as a friend. I will be an authentic friend because I want to have authentic friends. I will be loyal, honest, and trustworthy. I will be real with the guys in my life and allow them to be real with me. I will foster accountability and comradery. I will address offenses quickly and not let my ego get in the way of the growth that comes from healthy relationships.

I choose to MAN UP as a husband. I accept my wife for who she is, the way she is, and love her to the best of my ability. In my marriage, I will focus on what I have control over—me. I will pay attention to my wife's needs and support her in any way possible as I endeavor to lift her burdens and lighten her load in life. I will express my love for her in ways that are meaningful to her. I will keep communication open with her and always treat her as my equal partner. I will endeavor to make spending time with her alone a priority and always let her know how amazing she is. I will stay faithful to her and seek accountability if I am ever challenged in this area.

I choose to MAN UP as father. I will be fully present with my kids and look for ways to be the hero of their story. I will be honest and truthful with them even if it hurts me. I will teach them the value of hard work and set an example for the type of person they want to see and/or be in the future. I will discipline them in love with the goal to shape their character. I will make time for them, to play with them, to learn with them, to learn from them, and to simply enjoy life together.

I choose to MAN UP spiritually. I will take time to evaluate what I believe. I choose to be open. I choose to seek truth. I choose to forgive the past. I choose to live according to my beliefs and convictions. I will take the lead and set a spiritual example for my family and loved ones.

I choose to MAN UP for future generations. I choose to man up in every area of my life, spirit, soul, and body because I owe it to myself, my loved ones, and the world around me. I choose to be an authentic man and live as an authentic man because it's what the world so desperately needs now and in future generations. Today and every day, I rise to the challenge to MAN UP!

_____   _____

Signature   Date

_____

Witness

_____

Witness

ABOUT THE AUTHOR

Scott Schuler was raised around authentic, hardworking men, and at an early age developed a strong work ethic and drive to excel. He always had a passion and skill for helping others realize and achieve greatness from within, which ultimately led him to a career developing leaders as a highly successful professional in one of the fastest growing industries today.

The path wasn't always easy for Scott. Prior to becoming a chiropractor, his vocation for over a decade, he suffered from what he calls "Occupational A.D.D." Pressure from loved ones to pursue a white-collar career conflicted heavily with his passion for all things outdoors. For many years, Scott had no idea what he wanted to do. He bounced from occupation to occupation, following whatever seemed interesting at the moment, in hopes that something would eventually stick. This ranged from construction to veterinary work, landscaping to truck driving. He ultimately chose chiropractic because it seemed to be the best of both worlds—a "respectable" office job that also involved working with his hands. But still, Scott was dissatisfied which kept him open to exploring new opportunities. When his wife's at-home business started to thrive, and the income potential became clear, Scott knew he needed to shift his focus and take an active leadership role in the organization so he and his wife could develop what they had in their hands and grow it to the next level.

Scott was always a quiet observer of people. Over the course of his life and particularly while he was exploring different vocations, he noticed a common underlying theme among men that silently gnawed at him. Why weren't men banding together over a just cause like they used to? Why weren't they standing up for what they believed in like men once did? It was clear that somewhere along the way, men lost their strength to make decisions and stand up for themselves based on their values and morals instead of popular opinion. He mentally set this notion aside and stayed focused on his family and career, but it never went away.

While Scott was phasing out his chiropractic clinic and stepping into his new role, he found himself becoming more involved with the school activities of his three boys. As he attended field trips and extracurricular events, that gnawing observation resurfaced and was now glaring at him blindingly in the face. What he saw was the effects of this shift in men rippling out and putting the next generation at risk. It was clear that most boys today don't have a clue about what it means to be a man. What happened to the definition of manhood? How would this culture shift affect his own children? "I couldn't sit idly by watching males of all ages fumble around in search of direction and identity. Something had to be done and instead of complaining about it, I decided to MAN UP and do something about it."

With rousing support from his family and friends, Scott knew he needed to voice what was inside of him. This is the premise and inspiration for the book, "MAN UP" that issues the challenge to men to stand up for themselves, their beliefs, and for those who can't stand up on their own. It is a challenge to be authentic and to find resolve in every area of life.

Scott has been married to his wife Brenda for 21 years. They have three boys who share Scott's love for all things outdoors and anything that produces adrenaline. It is his hope that the lessons he learned throughout his life's experiences will serve as an example to them and to men everywhere on what it means to MAN UP.